TERRA NOVA
Global Revolution and the Healing of Love

by Dieter Duhm

ISBN 978-3-927266-54-4
First edition, © 2015 Verlag Meiga GbR
Monika Berghoff • Saskia Breithardt
Waldsiedlung 15 • D-14806 Bad Belzig
Tel. +49 (0) 33841 30538 • Fax: +49 (0) 33841 38550

info@verlag-meiga.org • www.verlag-meiga.org
Translated from German and edited by Martin Winiecki,
Dara Silverman, and Juliette Baigler
Original Title:
Terra Nova. Globale Revolution und Heilung der Liebe
Verlag Meiga, 2014

Table of Contents

Part III
THE WORLD CAN BE HEALED 93

Ecce Homo
Watercolor by Dieter Duhm

Acknowledgements

Foremost, I give thanks that it was possible to write this book at all, despite a bout of severe trigeminal inflammation. Gratitude also goes to my editor, Monika Alleweldt, for the loving support and patience with which she engaged with the manuscript. I give thanks for the English translation by Martin Winiecki, Dara Silverman, and Juliette Baigler. Thank you for the intelligent tenacity with which you insisted on certain changes in the book. I give thanks to my partner, Sabine Lichtenfels, who allowed me to write this book in her living room. She accompanied me with love and spent nights reading and editing the manuscript.

My gratitude reaches out to all friends and co-workers who have carried the project in recent years. To all those standing up against the global injustice. To all those who have dared a great deal until they were broken. To all those who have placed the justice of life above the written law. To the mothers and all women around the world who have persevered in spite of hunger, displacement, and torture – deep greetings and thank you. The movement continues – for our children, for life, for love, and for the liberation of all beings.

Foreword by the Author

As a student I regularly visited the Institute of Physiology at the University of Freiburg. From my window I saw a dog pen constructed from bare concrete. Dogs walked to and fro within it. I knew that they were designated for animal testing and that they awaited a horrible destiny. I decided not to engage with it and to simply suppress the issue in order to be able to study in calmness. I did what nearly everyone else did, but a bad feeling remained. In 2012, three million animals were sacrificed for animal testing in Germany alone. If we knew how rats, dogs, and monkeys suffer because of this, we would do anything to stop the horror. But it does not stop here, for everything that people do to animals they always at some point also do to other people. This book is meant to help put a definitive end to this insanity.

I was an activist in the 1968 student's movement. After the failure of the "new Left" in Germany, new approaches for the liberation from society's dead end needed to be discovered. As our ideological debates had come to their close, the question of the social, intrapersonal, ethical, and spiritual foundations of our work came into focus. How do we generate a new form of humaneness based on trust and mutual support? Where could the solution for the topics of sex, love, and partnership be found? How could the human community be integrated into the community of all beings and eventually into the order of the universe? Only if we succeeded in answering these questions, in the sense of profound peace work, could global healing be possible.

This book summarizes the thoughts and experiences made over nearly forty years of research on the topic of community. The education at the Tamera peace research center in Portugal emerged from the insights we developed. Every chapter can be read as an independent study unit; each contains a part of our approach to healing. Naturally, this is why some essential thoughts are repeated; with ever-new contexts, they shed light onto the necessary system change in our culture. This book was written for visitors and students coming to Tamera from around the world in order to understand the new system we have created here. Furthermore, it could open interesting perspectives for all seekers, both on a political and personal level. The book addresses renewal on a global scale and does not aim toward personal therapy. Only under the framework of a global healing concept can individual questions around healing, purpose, and the future be worked on with necessary depth. Not the individual, but all of humanity is trapped in a common trauma. The analysis of the *collective trauma* (see Glossary) gives rise to a new vision of healing.

The possibility of global healing is inherent to the fantastic possibilities within life itself. Etty Hillesum, a Jewish Dutch woman was twenty-nine when she was deported to a concentration camp. In her diary she wrote…

> *The misery is really big, but nevertheless, I often walk late in the evening when the day behind me has sunk away into profundity. I walk with whipping steps along the barbed wire and then it wells up out of my heart again and again – I cannot help it, it is the way it is, it is of an elementary power: life is something wonderful and big, later we have to build up a whole new world – and each further crime and each further cruelty we have to contrast with a further piece of love and goodness which we have to conquer within ourselves.*[1]

She wrote this in 1943, shortly before her death in the gas chamber. May this book contribute to fulfilling her legacy.

Introduction

We live in apocalyptic times. Through modern media we get an overview of what is happening on this planet, day by day. We see the miracles of technology, the high gloss of urban façades, the wealth of the elites; we see people beaten, hungry, and shot on all continents. We see how the outer layer of our planet, the biosphere, is being increasingly destroyed, and the out-of-control sprawl of monopolist economics exterminates ever more life in order to increase its profit. Currently most futurologists agree that human civilization needs a paradigm shift if we want to ensure our survival. To this end they think of new systems for energy, nutrition, urban living, societal organization, communication, markets, and finance. In addition, the development of digital technology brings new possibilities into view, all the way to the colonization of Mars – there seems to be no limit to futuristic fantasies.

One would love to join such "trips," were they not based on a fundamental flaw. The concepts almost exclusively address issues of the external world and ignore the much more fundamental issues of humanity's inner world. It is undoubtedly true: we need a paradigm shift to ensure future life on Earth. However this paradigm shift also encompasses our own way of thinking and the goals we set for ourselves. Today's human world is failing due not only to the flaws in society's structure and the economics of late capitalism; it is failing primarily due to the human being himself. The human being is the cause of his own failure because he disregarded some essential aspects of his own inner world. The inner world consists of the driving powers of his soul, his libidinous longings, his sexuality and animality, his spiritual powers, his hopes and fears, his entire potential of unrecognized and untapped energies. It is the inner workings of humanity that steer the external processes in politics and economics. Changes within the human being will determine whether a social revolution will be successful or not. This is why this book focuses mainly on inner transformation.

This analysis, that society and politics are based on a disregard for the true nature of the human being, applies more or less to the entire patriarchal epoch. This epoch was introduced with the construction of the Egyptian pyramids and with the intention of exercising imperialistic power. Since then, humanity has been building a system that can only be maintained by suppressing and eliminating essential aspects of the human soul, particularly the feminine aspects. Today this system works so perfectly that no opposition can measure up to it. And due to it more and more people, animals, and other fellow creatures perish every day. Behind the slogans of political parties and the boundless promises of the "happiness industry," hides the psychological suffering of a crumbling civil society. Hardly anyone can defend him or herself against a calamity that comes from within. Civil life has become an appendage to economic power systems that no one is able to fathom anymore. The times of democracy and free civil society are over; the resources are exhausted – an era comes to its close.

I am writing this book as spokesperson of the Tamera project in Portugal. This book contains the insights of forty years of research on the question: How can people live together and what kind of vision for a nonviolent world arises when they do? I do not describe the external form of the world to come, but its human foundations insofar as they have become visible in our work. It is not the technical, economic, and political image of a future society that is addressed, but its inner image – its sexual, social, ecological, ethical, and religious foundations. I want to show which inner regions of our human existence need to be explored in order to gain an understanding of the destruction of our culture and the possibilities for healing. As a project we started by working on community and found ourselves working with the issues of all humanity.

In order to explore the inner structures of a humane form of existence, we needed again and again to review and change the ways in which we coexisted. When we did the groundwork for what would become the community with a small group in 1978, we made a basic decision for our entire lives. I knew that from then on I needed to participate in all phases of community building in order to understand how group conflicts develop and how to dissolve them. I was a scientist and writer, but I needed experiential research training and this training has continued ever since. I have been spared nothing that happens among human beings. **If one wants to know how humankind functions, one should learn how a group functions, for a group contains all the light and shadow sides of our human existence within it.**

The outlines of a concrete utopia (see Glossary) formed ever more clearly through our continuous work in the community. Its global features are anchored in a new humaneness. In the area of sexuality and love above all, we found crucial keys for a core shift in the collective body of humanity. *"There cannot be peace on Earth so long as there is war in love,"* said the peace journalist Leila Dregger.[1] This is how the healing of love, especially the love between the genders, moved evermore to the center of our work.

The thoughts and visions described in this book revolve around the image of a new human civilization without fear and violence. We call it "Terra Nova." On this path, thrilling connections between the peaks of global vision and discoveries in interpersonal human relations came about. We need sensual and spiritual experiences in order to believe in a successful shift in global development. Spiritual and intellectual work is also required in order to assemble these experiences into a coherent image. I am aware that the image of Terra Nova presented here cannot be immediately manifested everywhere. We are undergoing an historical process, the result of which no one can predict. We can however give impetuses for a new direction. What seemed more important to me than Terra Nova's imminent applicability were the overall image and the direction of the great transformation that we are all undergoing.

The following chapters do not focus on the Tamera project, but rather the tenets of a humane revolution. One should not measure the truth of this book by how far we have come as a particular group. Even if new turbulence arises and hinders our development, the basic insights we have gained over many years will still be valid. The time is ripe. May many groups join all over the world. May the thoughts for the healing of love and care for all co-creatures come to life in a worldwide community. Terra Nova is the vision of a future world that has resolved the historic reasons for violence and war. May this book show this vision to be realistic.

PART I
APOCALYPSE AND CHANGE OF ERAS

Chapter 1: The Global Catastrophe

Innumerable human beings and animals die in too senseless and cruel a manner. Humankind, as well as the animal kingdom, is approaching global disaster: famine; catastrophes in water, energy, and climate; and the catastrophe in love. The calamity permeates both the material and psychological realms of life. War in the outer world and depression in the inner world are two aspects of the same development. The catastrophe rolls over the entire planet; the inferno comes closer. We are currently experiencing the collapse of the old systems and seeing almost all our hopes dashed. Billions of people are working every day for a system that they have not understood for a long time. They hear in the news about atrocities happening all around them, but they no longer believe in a solution for these problems. They seek out small, private niches where they can pursue their professions with minimal disturbance. Almost all of my former friends have sealed themselves off from the global reality through insulating themselves in a web of private relationships. The development of humanity has entered a dead-end that can no longer be overcome by conventional means. We are witnesses to a misguided civilization, to which we ourselves belong. The correction will not be achieved through accusations but by stepping out of the insanity of a culture that can only be maintained by killing more and more of our fellow beings, polluting more and more groundwater, eradicating more and more species, and exterminating more and more original life systems every day. It will also require of us the stepping out of old habits and the creation of a system of thinking that will serve as orientation for making belief and trust between us possible again.

Elementary values such as community, truth, solidarity, and compassion have been lost through millennia of war and the activities of global capitalism. The Earth's population lives under a hypnosis of fear and violence. The youth currently rising against the despotism of the old powers need a vision for a new world. All the adversities and struggles of our time highlight humanity's task of developing a convincing utopia and establishing planetary base stations for its manifestation. The Mayan date December 21, 2012 did not mark the end of humankind, but the beginning of a new era. The vision of a new interconnected world, as it is proclaimed by the digital prophets of Silicon Valley, is not wrong, but it urgently requires philosophical and ethical complementation if we are to make manifest the universal information pattern inherent to all beings, which enables a future without violence. This book is intended to further elucidate this.

Beyond All Tears

We who live in peace are constantly surrounded by a cruelty that we could not bear if we faced it directly. The structures of global capitalism have robbed hundreds of millions of people of their homes, their access to food, healthy drinking water, and a positive prospect for life. The methods with which wars are currently fought, dissidents tortured, news blocked, and witnesses killed are too cruel to be described. In addition there are strategies of global energy politics and globalized water management, which deprive the poor regions of Earth of their basic material resources. This development is systematic and will continue until we stop it or until it finds its ultimate end in a global holocaust of which we caught a glimpse in Fukushima, Japan in March 2011.

The pain of the world exceeds the scope of our comprehension. We can sympathize when we see the suffering of a dying animal in front of us, but we can no longer sympathize when we hear in the news of the great massacres of children, women, peoples, and animals every day. The worldwide barbarism has reached an unimaginable dimension. There is no public forum for the expression of this pain. There is no reverberation from the world to the death of young people in Syrian cities. Pain is especially horrible if there is no hope of relief.

The youth of the world look into a future without meaning and objective. This leaves them unable to make sensible use of their great potential for action. Moreover, they endure the collective experience of continuous betrayal, which results in the subconscious accumulation of hatred. A large proportion of young men around the world are presently living in "killer mode." They are trapped in a spiral of violence from which they can no longer liberate themselves. The epidemic of cruelty that is erupting everywhere on Earth today is the logical consequences of a system which could not possibly have been more diabolically contrived. Before we can conceive of the dimensions in which a global peace movement must work, we must recognize the dimensions of suffering in which many currently perish. In a German news magazine I read the following report about a Vietnamese girl forced into prostitution...

Sina Vann, [...], was kidnapped 12 years ago in her native Vietnam. Human traffickers smuggled her across the border to Cambodia, where Vietnamese women are in demand because of their light complexion – the whiter the skin, the higher the price. She woke up on a bed in Phnom Penh, drugged, naked and bleeding. Her virginity had been sold to a sex tourist for a few hundred dollars. She doesn't know where he was from. Then she was locked up, bound and beaten. She was sold as a virgin four or five more times, to Cambodian customers who didn't notice that her vagina had just been sewn shut – a common practice to ensure that the women bleed. She was tortured with electroshocks when she refused to service customers. The advantage of electroshocks is that they produce no visible damage that would reduce a girl's value.[1]

Do we still have feelings, thoughts, words with which we can adequately react to such savagery? It sounds like the most awful scene from a horror film but it is factual and it occurs on a daily basis! This is but one scene from the daily massacre on Earth – as quotidian as the abuse conducted in child pornography networks in all countries from Canada through Europe to Australia. Sexuality is one of the most atrocious crisis areas of our times. One among many. Those who direct their attention to the suffering of our fellow beings bear witness to a story that never ends. Behind the material consumption of our society stands the indescribable anguish of billions of our fellow beings. It stands behind the menus of our restaurants, the doctors' prescriptions, and the numbers on the stock market. The well-being of one side is achieved through systematic murder on the other. Countless human beings and animals pay with their lives for our daily intake.

We need to do something to categorically end these atrocities; we need to develop an idea, a plan, a global undertaking, for the liberation of life and all creatures. A plan for the liberation of love, a plan for a new humanity on a new Earth. This is how the Healing Biotopes Plan came into being – this is the basis of our work (see Part IV).

In the name of life.

In the name of love.

In the name of all beings.

Chapter 2: Revolution for Life

The plan developed over the course of the apocalyptic peaks that have occurred on the planetary stage since the 1970s. To put it briefly, it is the plan to found a new culture in alliance with all beings in the great family of life. It also attends to the inner nature of the human being, to its liberation from all suppression, and integration into the higher ethic of life. It is ultimately about finding an essential code for a humane civilization on our planet. The features of the plan are described more precisely in Part IV of this book, but first we want to shed light on some aspects of the current overall situation.

An inner contradiction permeates all of today's institutions – the contradiction between the laws of society and the laws of life, between *sociosphere* (see Glossary) and biosphere. The human being is a *Zoon Politikon* (see Glossary) – a societal being and as such is subject to the laws of society. However, in accordance with his physical and spiritual nature, he is at the same time a member of the "bio-cosmos" and is therefore subject to the laws of universal life. If these two laws contradict each other, disease, criminality, violence, and war arise. **Today we are experiencing the global culmination of this contradiction. We have come to an apocalyptic edge beyond which survival is no longer possible.**

What began in the Arab countries at the beginning of 2011 was a glimpse of a global war that could eventually erupt everywhere. The civil wars in the Arab countries will inevitably expand to the urban centers of the western world if we do not give this revolution a humane direction early enough. Oppressed life force rises up against their oppressors. We are experiencing a global battle between the powers of life and the forces of destruction. A highly organized syndicate of corporations, banks, lodges, secret services, and governments has enveloped the Earth in a network of exploitation and violence. Germany sends tanks to Arab countries, which can then be used on the whim of despots against protestors. Global capitalism has destroyed the last communities, the last loyalties, the last connections to home, humaneness, and ethics. Yet the epoch of capitalist globalization cannot continue without unimaginable bloodshed and without the destruction of nature on a massive scale, a fact banks and corporations know full well. Their Illuminati might want to consider waking up.

The world has broken open. The old systems are bursting; new powers are emerging which can no longer be contained. People everywhere are taking to the streets. They are protesting against a system that has broken its promises on all levels. The synthesis of these events gives rise to the call for a new concept of human life on planet Earth. We have slipped out of a higher order, the divine order of universal life, to which human being and nature equally belong. We call this the *Sacred Matrix* (see Glossary), and we have to find our way back to it. As grandiose as it may sound, this is the step we now need to take. We need a new fundamental order for our coexistence, and a new way of coexisting with all fellow beings. Two thousand years after Jesus Christ, seventy years after Auschwitz, and fourteen years after September 11th, we say with certainty: we need a new basis for life on our planet – new ethical, spiritual, scientific, social, sexual, ecological, technological, and economic foundations. Above all we need a new inner world from where the powers to create Terra Nova can emerge. This will not be achieved through the development of small, rural communes or urban groups so long as they are not embedded in a greater context. However, even the smallest groups, bookshops, and cafes can help to establish this greater context for Terra Nova.

The revolution can be won if it is grounded in the conviction in a positive goal. We need a revolution that accepts spirit, lust, and love, the right to life for all beings, and the right to humanity's religious longings. We need a revolution that helps the poor, the exploited, and the oppressed, the children, animals, and all creatures that so urgently need our assistance today. We thereby also help ourselves. This new revolution has to once again provide children with the experience of home, and it needs to acknowledge that even animals raised or bred for meat or fur production have a heart and a soul. Herein lies the deepest system change and the innermost core of the global drama. The need is not only for a change in political power; it is about fundamentally transforming our concept of a humane society. It is a matter of changing from murderous mechanics to compassionate solidarity and assistance. We need a revolution whose victory will create no losers because it will achieve a state that benefits all.

The term "revolution" is potentially problematic because it is immediately associated with violence. The current revolution will have to renounce all thoughts of violence if its humane goal is to be reached. Any revolution that originates from violence and war will only reiterate the old structures of brutality and domination; this is a lesson from history. **A humane goal cannot be reached through inhumane means. The end does not justify the means.** The current revolution is not a process of military confrontation but of mental and spiritual struggle. The structure and implementation of the new culture emerges

24

from mental and spiritual fields. (Instead of "revolution" we could speak of "transformation," as it has to do with a spiritual convergence. This convergence however is so radical that I have chosen the word "revolution.")

An essential theme of the current revolution, at its innermost core, is the issue of sexual love in connection with fundamental ethics of creation, the reunification of Eros and religion. Here religion no longer connotes affiliation to a faith group but the rediscovered life in unity with creation. Separated for thousands of years through dire moral doctrines from the world religions, Eros and religion need to come together again so that we human beings can rise up to the source from which all of life originates.

In order to end the spiral of violence we need to find an inner power that enables us to not retaliate against injustices we have suffered. The pilgrimages Sabine Lichtenfels guided through Colombia, Portugal, and Israel-Palestine were dedicated to this paradigm shift. "Grace" is what she calls the power that is "stronger than all violence."[1] We were very moved when we met a young woman in Israel whose face had been disfigured; she had been severely injured when a young Palestinian had carried out a suicide attack close to her. In her book, *Grace: Pilgrimage for a Future without War*, Sabine Lichtenfels describes the situation…

> *Three years ago she became the victim of a suicide-attack in a bus and by a miracle she survived. We had already met her here, years ago in the Jerusalem forest, a beautiful young woman. Now she sits here in our tent and talks. For two months she had lain in a coma and the doctors had given up on her. She fully understands the Palestinian suffering (…)*
>
> *Everyone listening is struck by her story. After intensive days in the West Bank where we have been made very aware of the suffering of the Palestinians, we now closely feel the experience of the other side. This young woman wanted nothing else but to live. Just like the Palestinians do. The soul has to understand anew: this is not so easy. It is not possible to divide the world into victims and perpetrators. Healing does not result from accusation. When she was asked about her feelings toward her tormentor she only said, "Maybe I would have done the same if I had been in his position."[2]*

On which side do we stand? Whosoever has decided for the side of life can no longer say "yes" to the habits he or she has hitherto mindlessly followed. If we have the courage to look at current world events, our entire organism reacts with an absolute "no!" Stop a system that does such things. Stop it also on the inside, in our own lives. This is the outcry of a healthy *emotional body* (see Glossary). But the world cannot be changed through emotions. Now the mind, the analyzing and synthesizing intellect, has to get involved in order to translate this emotional "no" into a positive helping strategy. With every small deed, every thought, and every decision we can consciously position ourselves on the side of life. Through our daily actions, we are weaving a web with which we strengthen one or the other side. While washing dishes we can decide *"whether we serve the devil or the Lord."*[3]

Stop the Global Idiocy

Countless millions of young people all around the globe would be available for building a new world if they were offered a credible vision to work toward. Yet they hardly ever find opportunities to express their humane potential. Before they can become conscious of their power, their energy is programed and channeled in the logic of the existing systems. They are being used as henchmen of the system to solve conflicts they have not caused. There are only very few people at the top of the societal pyramid that give the orders, as exemplified by those behind the FIFA World Cup 2022 in Qatar. How many human lives are being sacrificed here for an insane economic deal! And the world just watches. In fact, after 150 years of democracy and civil rights it is still small groups of powerful people that steer the destiny of billions. We can hardly believe this story while we stand inside of it, but when we take sufficient distance we see the boundless despotism that still directs human society on all continents.

Fall 2013 – In Istanbul young policemen are on a full combat mission against protestors of the same age. Everywhere in the world we see the same idiotic theater. Everywhere two hostile camps of young people confront each other, people that could actually be friends. Enemies that could actually be friends! We must not allow hostilities to arise purely on the basis of affiliation to different ideologies and political camps. This primitive mentality should have ended with playing "Cowboys and Indians" in our childhood. It is not personal hatred that makes people enemies but the logic of a distorted system. Enough! Stop this whole insanity! There is an alternative. Another life is possible. There exists another plan of creation for all of us. We are not here to fight each other but to build the world we need for our children and ourselves. We must join with all those who stand for peace, against war, against any form of hypocrisy, and against distorting or concealing reality. We can no longer avert our gaze from what is really happening to the victims, be they in Syria or the nearby supermarket. We have friends in Palestine and Israel, in Colombia and Mexico. The children, the friends, the beloved ones that are dying in this moment could be our own. Whoever has heard their cries will never forget them. **This war will persist everywhere so long as the societal structures that perpetuate it remain.**

During a demonstration in Sao Paulo a policeman throws his pistol into the fire saying, "Enough! I will no longer participate in this."[4] Together with his colleagues he was supposed to proceed against the demonstrators; he could not continue because he knew justice was on their side. Justice was on the side of the demonstrators; injustice was on the side of the government. Like everywhere in the world, the police have the task to protect the system from its indignant citizens. This is how injustice is protected, often by military means. This is how every revolution begins. Yet the police also consist of young people, as young and likable as the protestors. The police officers know, at some level, that justice is on the side of the protestors; more and more of them know it, but they have to do their job and earn money; they do not yet have another perspective. The protestors will also one day, when they have lost the battle, return to their old places and do their "jobs." Let us be sure that they will gain another perspective!

What would happen if they really had an alternative perspective – the vision of a society free from injustice and violence? The vision of a society in which they all have enough to eat without needing to obey unjust laws? The vision of a world where they, especially women, could love freely and without censure? What would happen if the millions that are currently demonstrating on the streets and in the squares had a clear vision and started to manifest it? We would experience the real emergence of a free world with functioning communities and subsistence economies, with love couples free from the fear of punishment, with free religion, and free culture. We would have schools for learning the secrets of life, research sites for new communication systems, new architecture, new energy systems, new housing arrangements, new water landscapes with alimentary biotopes, new healing methods, a new coexistence with animals; we would have Love Schools to teach new ways for the genders to meet and new "monastery" schools for cooperation with the spiritual world. Everywhere on Earth, in all countries, on all continents, the new projects will arise. Young police officers will no longer fight against protestors, but will ally with them to create the new world. A world that is currently closer than ever before because we have the knowledge to make it happen.

System Change in Our Own Bodies: Diseases of Transformation

The world is in transformation. Transformation is the conversion of mental and spiritual systems. We are at the end of an historic (patriarchal, imperialistic, capitalistic) epoch and at the beginning of a new one; we are human beings in transition. We live suspended between the old and the new era. The upcoming system change will also occur within us. When old and new energy fields collide within the human organism it can cause disease patterns to arise in our bodies. Here we are speaking of "diseases of transformation."

All psychosomatic illnesses, headaches, joint pain, skin diseases, coordination disturbances all the way to Parkinson's can be diseases of transformation that heal by themselves as soon as a solution reveals itself within the organism. We experience this difficult transition time on many different levels: from the spiritual problems of finding meaning, to personal problems in love or work, all the way to the global ecological and political problems. Many problems, conflicts, and hardships from which we have hitherto suffered privately – because we believed we needed to solve them individually – do not originate from a personal deficiency, but from an objective global situation that calls for total change. We need new thinking and new knowledge that shows us the way out. It has been a founding thought of the Healing Biotopes Project (see Part IV) to concentrate as much of this knowledge as possible in a single place in order to open the mind and spirit to the possibilities of comprehensive healing work. We needed to see the image in order to believe in its manifestation. Such a place arises in southern Portugal.

Chapter 3: Collective Trauma – The Morphogenetic Field of Fear

Behind the crisis of our time hides the core crisis of human relationships. Behind the atrocious massacres, which are currently (as of 2014) epitomized in Syria, hides a collective soul pattern, which seems to be consistent on all continents. It is a pattern of fear. In the background of our civilization lies the *morphogenetic field* of fear (see Glossary). From this field arise horrific forms of cruelty that are actually attempts to kill off one's own inner fear. If we want to generate lasting peace on Earth we need to transform this pattern of fear into a basic pattern of trust. This is easily said but the fear is deeply anchored within our cells. It has become a firm component of our genetic and physiological makeup; it operates as an unconscious reflex. *"Fear has to vanish from the Earth,"* Mikhail Gorbachev said. I do not know if he knew the profundity of this statement, however he named the deepest and most comprehensive goal we face today if we want to give a humane direction to evolution. The goal of healing work is to enable a life free from fear. The morphogenetic field of fear needs to be replaced entirely by a morphogenetic field of trust.

Fear is the result of the last millennia. Walter Schubart, in his book *Religion und Eros*, wrote that there is an original fear at the base of all psychological suffering – the fear of separation. It is the fear of separation that prompts us toward the most insane acts. Separation from our home, family, love partner, group – is there not something that is the same in all these fears, a primal fear of separation? It is difficult to convey the deepest, most primal layers of the soul in words. Time and again, generation after generation, the human being has been separated from that which his original nature most loves, what he loves like a child, simply because he is human, a breathing, sensual, living being. We have fallen away from the oneness and are not finding the way back. We live in "banishment," as Friedrich Weinreb put it. Healing would thus mean reconnecting humanity with its actual home. This is the *entelechial* (see Glossary) direction of our evolution at present – reintegrating the human world into its original home in life, in love, within the precepts of the Sacred Matrix.

Fear is not a private problem; it is the psychological consequence of a civilization gone awry. It arose in the collective cruelties of humanity. The task of global peace work entails the dissolution of the collective trauma, which accumulated in the collective subconscious of humanity throughout thousands of years of war and expulsion, treachery and betrayal.

Do we know that our entire culture, our states and nations have originated from war? Every one of today's states exists on conquered land on which there were once indigenous people; there were faithful people, love couples, and playing children. The United States of America needed to eradicate native tribes and enslave millions of Africans to be able to build their nation. Truly these are not good conditions for building a humane civilization. The economy of western countries is fuelled by, among other things, the weapon industry and arms trade. This is how normal war has become; how thoughtlessly we have become accustomed to it! War has become a fixture of our society. We live in a "war society" which economically cannot afford peace. If our western societies were to abandon the war economy, millions would lose employment. They could all help to establish a new peace-based economy.

Our civilization is dominated by a profound idiocy, a veritable disease of mind and spirit. It does not fit within life's plan for people to willfully shoot at each other; this is not coherent with the code of a humane world. War is the result of an inconceivable aberration. When it is claimed that war has "always existed," we respond that it is time to end this historic insanity. As of now, war must have no place in human culture just as jealousy has no place in love. Have we really needed thousands of years to discover this simple truth? It will be unfathomable to our descendants that people have killed each other out of jealousy. They will understand even less how people could have shot at each other and perpetrated far worse cruelties. It is no use referring to the violence in the animal kingdom or to quote Heraclitus, *"War is father of all things."*[1] Such reasoning rests on the assumption that the world should remain as it has "always been." Those who argue thus fail to see the Creator's power within humankind and the potential for transfiguration. We are certainly not the product of the past, nor are we determined by natural laws. We are the creators of our lives. We have the freedom and the task to build a better world and it will function if it corresponds to the rules of the Sacred Matrix. Here I want to quote Satprem, a student of the Indian philosopher Sri Aurobindo and the Mother from Auroville. He writes...

> *After breaking through all those evolutionary layers, you suddenly emerge, in the depths of the body, into something where the old laws of the world no longer have power. And you realize that their power was nothing but a huge*

collective suggestion – and an old habit. But just a habit! There are no "laws"; there are only fossilized habits. And the whole process is to break through those habits. (...) But that state has to come to a point when it's experienced spontaneously and naturally by the body, which means freeing it of all its conditioning. Then you emerge into something fantastic. But really fantastic! Although I suppose that the first gliding of a bird in the air also was fantastic. Yet there was a moment when an old reptile took off and became a bird.[2]

There are no ready-made laws and no ultimate physical laws pertaining to our bodies. There are only entrenched behavioral habits and there is a freedom within ourselves that enables us to rise to a higher form of life.

When we shed light on the vileness encapsulated within the word "war," we see the pictures of horror stored in the inherited memory of humankind, pictures of mass murder, mutilation, fleeing, and hunger. These experiences have repeated generation after generation, over hundreds and thousands of years. They have been deeply carved into humanity's genetic memory. Our collective human soul is burdened with this nightmare.

There is buried within us all a traumatic shell; it can explode at any time. *"Everyone has their Vietnam,"* said Claude AnShin Thomas, a war veteran and Buddhist monk, who has wandered the world working for peace.[3] What is currently happening in the outbursts of violence – in gang fights and youth prisons, in schools, neighborhoods, football stadiums, and torture chambers – is the consequence of a global trauma that will continually repeat until the root causes are eradicated once and for all.

Originating from a long history of war, these horrific images form the **traumatic core** of humanity. This traumatic core exercises a subconscious tyranny over the basements of the soul, fires images of fear into our organism, betrays love, ridicules faith, produces patterns of negative interpretation of all events, and fights people who think differently. It produces erroneous notions of disease and healing; it steers our psychosomatic processes, our perceptions, and reflexes, our hormones, our nerve function, and muscle contractions. We are subconsciously attuned to the informational matrix of the trauma. We live in the subconscious scenario of omnipresent danger against which we need to defend ourselves. The world appears to be an anonymous jury before which we need to protect and justify ourselves. There is a collective feeling of being judged. Behind all psychological malformation, all forms of neurosis and psychopathy, hides the big collective trauma, a disease affecting the entire human race.

I want to quote Eckhart Tolle. He refers to the collective trauma as the "pain-body." He writes…

> *This energy field of old but still very much alive emotion that lives in almost every human being is the pain-body. The pain-body, however, is not just individual in nature. It also partakes of the pain suffered by countless humans throughout the history of humanity, which is a history of continuous tribal warfare, of enslavement, pillage, rape, torture, and other forms of violence. This pain still lives in the collective psyche of humanity and is being added to on a daily basis, as you can verify when you watch the news tonight or look at the drama in people's relationships.*[4]

We have grown accustomed to horrific news; it has enveloped us in fog. In the moment of awakening, a strange thought hits us: Can it all be true? Have we really participated in it? And, how do we get out? It is barely possible to see through the mechanisms inherent within the existing society and still continue walking the old path. Do we have to step out? If so, how? Where to? In order to be able to step out, we need an alternative to step into. It does not yet exist in its finished form, but arises through the creation of centers for cultural transformation, birthplaces of a new Earth. The collaboration of hundreds, thousands, millions is now needed for building the new structures, new working places, and new professions required for creating Terra Nova. All those who still have a meaningful function in the existing society may use it for setting the course toward Terra Nova. The revolution needs not only radical activists but also mediators between the old and new world.

In the wake of the great trauma, disturbances emerge in interpersonal communication. In almost all cases, they run according to a similar pattern of subconscious belief sentences that constantly perpetuate the latent subliminal war among people.

I want to name three examples:

1. Many people live in the subconsciously imagined situation of not being accepted by others. Consequently, they interpret the reactions of those they speak with from this vantage point. A compliment can thus be heard as ironic, a pensive gaze as judgment, a question as aggression, a good

suggestion as criticism, and so on. This is how severe interference emerges beneath the surface of our contacts; this is seldom understood and can lead us all the way to hatred. In many political discussion groups one witnesses conversations that become increasingly long and meaningless, for they are steered by the distress of subconscious beliefs that have absolutely nothing to do with the objective issue at hand. Such neurotic interpretation patterns become especially dire in love relationships. Once two lovers have worked themselves into the noose of such misunderstandings there is rarely a way out because any rational possibility for correction is shut down. How many relationships fail due to the injuries partners inflict upon each other from within the interpretation pattern of non-acceptance? And once they are really at odds with each other the assumption of non-acceptance finds obvious confirmation. This is a stark example of a self-fulfilling prophecy. The neurotic then has every reason to see his delusion as reality. He defends himself against everything that could heal him. In fact this is a fundamental problem of our society – a deep psychologically anchored defense against anything that could heal.

2. A second example, closely related to the first, is the fear of separation in love. As a result of the great trauma many people live with the conviction of not being loved. When they have found a love partner they still tacitly do not believe in his or her love and therefore live in latent mistrust and latent fear of loss. They therefore do everything to prevent separation, which is exactly how they invoke actual danger of separation. For the strategies one enacts within the fear of separation – such as clinging, whining, complaining, blackmailing, etc. – are not conducive to love. As a therapist, I have witnessed this pernicious pattern of self-fulfilling prophecy to be present in almost all love relationships. It is not easy to believe in love within a society whose sexual laws force most people to lie to their partner. The therapeutic response ultimately consists of building a community where no one has to lie anymore.

3. An astonishing example of the impact of subconscious paradigms is provided in the history of the First World War. All nations that started the war –Germany, Austria-Hungary,

Russia, and France – lived under the expectation of immanent attack by one of the others – a typical relict of the great historic trauma. Historians agree that there was no rational reason for war. It was a psychological theater beyond compare. One could have performed it on stage with humor, had not approximately fifteen million people died. This is a classic example of the psychopathological background to global politics so long as it is directed by people that have not resolved their subconscious trauma.

I am trained as a psychoanalyst and have actually never left this profession, but I have continued, deepened, and refined it over almost forty years of group work. In order to understand what happens among human beings, I needed to get to know many layers of the soul: the conscious and unconscious, open and suppressed, biographic and karmic layers. I have gotten to know more than a hundred groups and projects and have seen how the same basic patterns of neurosis recur everywhere in similar form. I myself have been my best research object; bit-by-bit the psychological processes, the habitual reactions and disguises, the suppressed images and impulses, which comprise the totality of the subliminal war of our times, revealed themselves. The war was also latently in me. However, there was an inner point from which I could recognize and correct my neuroses. We call it the "God Point" in the human being. It is the inner point of reflection from which we receive direct feedback that enables us to remain on the entelechial track. I assume that it exists in all people. It is implicit then that everyone would be able to recognize their mental incapacity and live a responsible life.

A very important condition for successful global healing work is the dissolution of the traumatic core. With this realization we stand outside of all historic revolutionary concepts. We need ways of living that enable us to overcome our horrible heritage. Generating such ways of living is the crucial topic of our time. One immediately understands that a phenomenon is addressed here that can neither be solved by political revolution nor by individual therapy. We need collective solutions, a healing of the psychological foundations.

From our many years of healing work, we know how difficult it is to dissolve the psychological consequences of this trauma. The groups currently standing on the political and human frontlines need an extensive knowledge of life and its healing powers if they are to withstand the conflict. We can activate the powers of healing with every action. The work in the new centers is largely and fundamentally consciousness work. It requires collective training to continuously choose the positive side. The old field of anger and fear has to be transformed, through an historic effort, to a field of trust and love. We have to do this with all our strength, in collaboration with all peace groups and projects worldwide, **until the information of peace has become firmly absorbed into the genetic system of Homo sapiens.**

Chapter 4: Destroyed Love

The brutality of thousands of years of violence has shattered love. No area has been destroyed more horribly. Behind the misery of our civilization stands the collective misery in love. Millions of young love couples find no way out of their pain because they live in a system which offers no escape. They love each other then they desire someone else then they have to lie to each other and then the hatred looms over them. **They start to hate what they once loved. Eventually they no longer believe in love and need to compensate for their deep frustration through mindless consumption and all the things that cause the world to perish. War is one such compensation. This is the tragedy of our times.** The conventional habits of life and consumption conceal a tragedy in love. Children are infected by this; they become mistrusting, withdrawn, or criminal. Extreme criminals often had loveless families. Today's society has had to put into effect many measures to handle the crimes that stem from despair in love. **The global peace movement will only be able to overcome the powers of destruction once it has created a credible alternative in the area of love.** Herein lies the most difficult and most important foundational work to which the Tamera project has committed itself from the very beginning. This is also the work that has to date found little recognition in the world, yet it must be understood for a meaningful conversation to begin.

Today the pain of failed love is imprinted as collective information into the code of life in all people. Many so strongly protect themselves from this pain returning that they even eradicate the memory of love from their inner life. One no longer knows what one speaks about when speaking about love. Here we touch a deep drama in human history. Perhaps it is even deeper in women than in men because the feminine soul is especially connected with suppressed life. Woman's sexual hope could never be realized while the male world continued to abuse body and life. Through the research in our Healing Biotope we see how much the feminine begins to blossom when it is no longer forced into sexual hypocrisy.

The Hammer of the Witches

In order to institute its power in church and state, the patriarchal world needed to suppress sexuality and subjugate the woman under laws of male dominance. The obedience of woman was seen as a condition for male potency. A disastrous connection was formed between sex and power. Women that did not obey were punished or eliminated, like Hypatia of Alexandria and many others. In many countries the violence of man against woman took on unimaginable dimensions. The *Hammer of the Witches,* a book published in 1487, called for the murder of all women other than those necessary for reproduction. This book, written by two monks, soon became the second most read book in Germany after the Bible. One has to hear this a couple of times in order to actually believe it. As a consequence women who stood out for their attractiveness or intelligence, their independent will or courage, were slandered as witches and burned alive. Burned alive!

This is still happening in many countries today – stoning, burning, maiming, acid attacks. The victims are most often women.

Mary Magdalene

Suppressing female sexuality was and is a fundamental condition for patriarchal power and domination. All patriarchal cultures, no matter how different they otherwise might be, are consistent in their sexual suppression of women. When King Cecrops introduced monogamy in Greece in the middle of the second millennium BCE, it applied only to woman.[1] It was a barbaric slash into woman's sexual nature. Woman, by nature deeply connected to physical love, was meant henceforth to belong to only one man. What currently appears to many as the noble image of marriage is the result of an historical process that was forced upon women through the most atrocious means.

The magnitude of the male world's need to assert its power over women – in order to affirm its own position – revealed itself in an event in Rennes-le-Château, a tiny mountain village in southern France. The story revolves around the village priest, Bérenger Saunière. While excavating beneath the altar of the village church, he found a treasure that brought him a lot of money. It supposedly consisted of centuries-old, original manuscripts that exposed a love relationship between Jesus and Mary Magdalene and the likelihood that they even bore a child together. This discovery so blatantly breached church doctrine that before long public dignitaries came to the priest to offer him a great sum in exchange for the documents. This developed into one of the most surreal crime stories of the past century, involving many deaths. Were it the case that Jesus did in fact have a sexual love relationship with Mary Magdalene, the entire ecclesiastic doctrinal system of chastity, fornication, and hell would collapse. When sensual love is allowed, the power of sexual taboo, as the most important means for taming and controlling, is neutralized. Were this development to lead toward *free love* (see Glossary), humanity would become completely ungovernable. This is what tyrants in state and church sensed, with their unmistakable instinct for power. Masonic fights, religious wars, the burnings of books and heretics, the legends relating to Leonardo da Vinci all revolved around the issue of the sexuality between Jesus and Mary Magdalene. It became a political matter, which perhaps had a greater impact on occidental religious culture than any other!

Thank You to the Women

Once one has perceived the suffering of women, one is astonished that there could still be women capable of love. This is a crucial point and here I would like to thank the entire female gender. The female half of humanity must possess a very stable and faithful heart, faithful to the male half, which abused and suppressed it for thousands of years.

Even today there is still a long way to go before we actually achieve so-called "equal rights." In the sexual area in particular, very different standards apply; when a man in the public eye has a sexual escapade it is considered a trivial offence. When a female public figure does it, it is a scandal.

When we look back on our cultural history we can see the insanity in its entirety. Man has humiliated woman and thereby destroyed himself. He desecrated Eros and in doing so has driven himself over the edge. Generation after generation, century after century he has issued false propaganda demanding the demonizing of the flesh, the chastising of children, and the burning of witches. Originally designated for love and joy, physical lust became cause for ostracism and persecution. People began denying that which they had formerly loved. To this day our culture suffers from this perversion of values. **The lust of the flesh has been denounced as fornication and eliminated through the cruelest of means. No truth has been possible since. It is not the lust of flesh, but its suppression which is humanity's original sin.**

Fulfilled Eros and fulfilled love (not cybersex) are conditions for human happiness, cornerstones of a *concrete utopia,* and indispensible foundations for a future without war. When sex and love remain unfulfilled, frustration develops; frustration leads to subliminal aggression, which eventually erupts. At the core of many marital conflicts we find the unacknowledged anger of the woman who for decades had to hide her sexual needs behind the disguise of love and service.

Change of Thinking

When we understand the extent to which human society has succumbed to collective trauma in the area of sexual love it becomes clear why, in the name of global healing, the founders of our project needed to focus so much attention on "issue number one." This provoked the most terrible slander against us from the German public – accusations of "sexism," being a "sex-cult," "misogyny," "pornography," and even "child abuse." The defamations in the media were limitless. One alleged the exact opposite of what we actually said and did – "Dieter Duhm preaches violence against children," was the headline in a Protestant church bulletin. All of our project leaders were banned from speaking at public events. Engagements, which had already been confirmed, were cancelled on short notice; posters were defaced with fascist slogans and journalists who wanted to make positive reports about us were blocked by their editors. We had no chance to stand up for ourselves. I had not known that something like this was still possible in Germany. We had to persevere until the first walls of resistance and slander were brought down. Now, as the whole world faces collapse, our work can re-emerge in a new light.

At the end of the 1960s I was one of the activists in the German students' movement, until I ultimately saw that we could no longer change the world with Marxist concepts. I realized that the destruction within human relationships was stronger than the external constraints. One night a comrade of ours collapsed in the pub while drinking a beer; he had been poisoned by friends who regarded him as a traitor. This was the moment I jumped from this train. In the early seventies countless apartment shares and communes broke apart under the burden of unresolved human conflicts. These fights centered mostly on sex and love, authority and money. It was not political but basic human problems that led to the failure of these groups. The conclusion was clear: we need a new direction of thinking that can give an answer to the external **and** internal devastation. The private issue must become a political one. **The most intimate questions of sex, love, and partnership, of faithfulness, trust, and community, of jealousy, competition, and fear of separation are political questions with global implications.** The switch to our private decisions, which we hold in our hand, is now no longer a private switch but is connected with all of humanity. The way we deal with our anti-authority, social, and sexual problems is of political importance. Political engagement for peace is unquestionably linked with new ethical decisions in our human relations. There can be no peace in the world so long as we conduct secret wars among each another for power and sex. **Vibrant communities are necessary for effective peace work, communities that rediscover and manifest fundamental human values such as truth, trust, solidarity, and mutual support.** For those who seek a humane association for the term "socialism," this acknowledgement transforms the concept of socialist revolution. It was insights such as these that eventually, after many steps, led to the establishment of the Tamera project.

A deep change occurred in our consciousness. The goals of a socialist society that we had propagated in the New Left of the sixties could not be achieved without thoroughly overcoming humanity's traumatic core. The war raging in the outer world could not end so long as an inner war continually destroyed our solidarity and love relationships. When the heartache is stronger than the revolutionary goal, one remains attached to one's problems instead of solving them. So long as the inner conflicts remain unresolved, no sustainable success will be achieved externally. In order to reach something of a sustainable global and individual healing, we needed to discover pathways for ending the inner war. This was a critical insight but the attempt to integrate the healing of our **inner world** into political work was so new that there were no role models to guide us. Karl Marx did not have this work in sight. He did not know how he could give a political interpretation to his desire for his housekeeper.[2] The global political stage is full of such episodes, for it is enacted by people and all people share the same basic topics. Perhaps it is still the case today that the big political decisions of the world are steered more by small sexual episodes and wishes than by reason. Putin, who scorns sexual perversions of all kinds, gifted his Italian friend Berlusconi an expensive double bed. What an endorsement between men and what cheeky hypocrisy to say one thing and do another!

During the German students' revolution, I coined the phrase, *"Revolution without emancipation is counterrevolution."*[3] It was published in 1968 as the headline of a widely distributed pamphlet. Everyone spoke about it but hardly anyone knew what implications it would hold for one's private and political way of life. The members of our community needed to risk a lot and make many mistakes in the first years of the project until a convincing path became clear. We needed to work through our own resistances and through the fore mentioned public slander, cult accusations, and sanctions. I myself abandoned love through this. At this point I want to ask for forgiveness from all of my former companions who were hurt due to my anger and my own deep-rooted fear structure. It is unbearable how many injuries we inflict upon each another – often with the best intentions – due to the subconscious interpretation of our surroundings as hostile. This interpretation becomes self-perpetuating, a self-fulfilling prophecy, if we do not recognize and correct it. The *hologram* (see Glossary) of hostility and fear projections has to vanish from the emotional bloodstream of future peace workers if we are to create a social platform that will assure success. This platform consists of the unconditional solidarity among all those who are fully committed to achieving peace.

Chapter 5: The Birth of a New Era

We live not only in a world of increasing barbarism, but also in times of change in which more and more powers of renewal become visible. It is with astonishment and joy that we learned that even Pope Francis no longer attacks individual aspects of capitalism but the entire system, declaring the dominant economic model to be *"unjust from its roots,"*[1] emphasizing *"such an economy kills."*[2] As the message of revolution has now reached even the Vatican, other elites could also start to rethink their position.

The dream of a new world is not only a subjective wish, but also an authentic matrix for a different life, anchored in the structures of reality; it is an objective necessity and a possibility. The concrete utopia is a latent reality within the universe, just as the butterfly is a reality latent within the caterpillar. It lies in the structure of our physical and biological world, in our genes, and in our deeper ethical orientation. Within the context of committed peace work is not the fixing of individual defects within existing structures that is required; what is required is a fundamental system change. Today's societal machine will not be rectified by changing individual components, because the whole machine was wrongly constructed in the first place.

To reverse from this dead-end we do not need megacities or trillion dollar technologies to enable the colonization of Mars, as interesting as this might be; **we need intelligent concepts for cohabitating planet Earth anew.** We do not need reform; we need a new direction for human evolution. We are likely at the beginning of the greatest revolution in history. It is a planetary process, the outcome of which is still uncertain. As humankind sent a fully functioning shuttle, equipped with a digital laboratory, to Mars, it could also develop a new concept for a nonviolent planetary existence. In the following chapters components of such a concept will be proposed.

An initial, fundamental, and universally applicable condition for a humane future can be stated immediately: the new way requires the reintegration of human existence into the basic laws of life, community, love, and the Earth. To this also belong ethical, social, and ecological laws. **Any violence we inflict upon fellow beings will, in the long run, return to us as disease or insanity. The coming civilization is free of any cruelty. Plants and animals are our cooperation partners for creating a new way of living on Earth.** The laws of societal life and the laws of creation need to unite in order for global healing to occur. There is the world that we create and there is the world that has created us. These two worlds must come together. That is the goal of the journey.

To enable us to do the work of global healing we above all require two sources of life: healthy water and vibrant love. Water is to nature what love is to the human being. Through healing water, we cure nature; through healing love, we cure humankind. The healing of water and the healing of love equally demand that existing societal systems be turned upside down (Latin root: "revolution"). In both areas we observe that the same basic laws of life are in contradiction with the basic laws of capitalism. The new era develops to the degree that the basic laws of life are discovered, perceived, and followed by humanity.

To enable us to pave the way to a humane future, we need convincing models. These would show how human coexistence could be anchored in the universal energy fields of life. Once a functioning model is set up somewhere – a living model for ending the war between the genders, for the healing of love, for the cooperation with nature, and the solidarity with all fellow beings – a new reference point becomes available in the international discussion. The peace projects around the world have a new basis to think and speak from. It is like a quantum leap in political thinking. To enable this we must increase our concentration on the inner work, for it is the inner human world from which conflict and war originates. The more deeply we understand the global issues, the more deeply we recognize our own part in them. The rudiments of everything that we lament in the world can be found within ourselves, in our own lifestyle and community, even among friends. So long as the inner structures are not cleansed of the barbarism of the past, we will continue to reproduce the barbarism externally. **To put it bluntly, so long as there is lying, betrayal, fear, and violence in love, militaries, the arms industry, and trade in weaponry will continue to exist.** We are incongruent when we join protests for peace while we are full of (secret) hatred. When we begin to love the community we live in, we will find this community changed and more beautiful the very next day. **Whether the external world reacts peacefully or violently toward us largely depends on the thoughts and feelings with which we meet it.** Thoughts of loathing or revenge – no matter how subtle and secret – generate fear, violence, and war. With every thought of hope and reconciliation we deprive war of its fuel. In this way we participate every day in the birth of a new era. We have to create ways of living whereby we are ready and willing to achieve this transformation in ourselves.

Marx was right when he said that it is societal conditions that determine consciousness; he failed however to see that exactly these societal conditions were created by human consciousness. What else could have created them? It is the "subjective factor" – the inner world of thoughts, images, and impulses – which generates everything that we then see as a finished product in front of us. It is logical then that if we want to change these results we need to change consciousness, i.e. the inner world. Healing Biotopes are centers for this change of consciousness, nuclei of crystallization for global transformation.

Universal consciousness today leads us to a new model of life where the basic values of human existence – values such as truth, love, and solidarity, home, faithfulness, and belief – can be taken up on a new, reflected, and autonomous level. There is an inherent sacredness of life and a corresponding mental, spiritual, and ethical order which we must not ignore, even if it has been terribly misused by church and state, and extremely so under fascism. We need communities in which we consciously and purposefully coexist with the sacred powers of the universe and love. **Healing means reconnecting with the original energy field of life. This applies to the individual organism, the organism of a community, and the organism of all humanity.**

Can the World Still be Saved?

Many attempts to heal this world have been made to no avail but to the contrary. Maybe we have never had so much pain around the world. Maybe there has never been so much death, so much grief, and at the same time such a great lack of empathy. The ubiquity and intensity of the pain in the world exceeds our capacity for empathy.

Can the world still be saved? Can this Earth still be healed? Is there a realistic chance for a future without war? Today such questions are usually received with wry smiles rather than taken seriously. Current debates on change and reform for a better world start mostly with the premise that certain fundamental structures within politics and economics have the character of natural constants and therefore cannot be modified. Terms such as "market," "yield," "bank," or "military budget" have become part of the holy mantra of the system and cannot be questioned. From their outset, attempts at reform operate within narrow confines and little space for structural change remains.

Can the world still be saved? The acclaimed author Naomi Klein answers, *"Absolutely. Is it possible without challenging the fundamental logic of deregulated capitalism? Not a chance."*[3] So it is. **To understand how and why, under the aforementioned**

circumstance, salvation is nonetheless possible, we have to step out of the old categories of political thinking and enter into realms of thought shaped by different information and other parameters. While in its current state of damage the world seems to have as little or as much chance of healing as a person who, according to doctors, suffers an "incurable disease." Yet we have innumerable case studies of so-called miracle healings. Beyond the parameters of conventional medicine, there obviously also exist very different laws and powers of salvation. In addition to his physical body, the human being possesses another body, which for simplicity I will just refer to as the *spirit body* (see Glossary). It works according to different laws than the material body. If we succeed in introducing the right information into the spirit body, our entire organism would change instantly. If I for example tell a shy person how courageous he is, different hormones are immediately released. We receive information through the spirit body and corresponding guiding impulses are conveyed instantaneously into the physical body. Could the same that applies to the individual organism not also pertain to the global organism? The overall organism of humanity would thus possess a spirit body (the *noosphere* – see Glossary) functioning according to principles other than those in the material body. If new information is entered into the noosphere the whole world changes. This is the basic hypothesis of Tamera's Political Theory. The world could of course still be saved if we enter the corresponding information into its system.

The Universal Human Being

When the relations between humankind and the world are no longer blocked by fear and mistrust, new channels of perception, new contact to nature, and new feelings for all living beings come to fruition. With the newly gained trust the human being recognizes his inner connection to the environment and to all that has body and soul. A new worldview concretely emerges in which the human being has a new position within the whole of creation. The human being experiences himself as a responsible member of the great family of life. By virtue of his cognition he becomes the thinking organ of life, or as Julian Huxley put it, the *"eye of evolution."*[4] This is how he can recognize and direct development.

Once the inner blockages are removed, we see that the currents of life that flow through love also flow through water in clouds and in the growth of plants. There is an essential universal energy which is steered not only by physical processes but also through our thoughts and actions. We have the task to guide this universal energy correctly – for the benefit of all beings. This energy has been wrongly directed throughout many thousands of years of war, which is how an energetic entity of violence and fear formed on Earth. The morphogenetic field of fear has steered human life generation after generation, until it was seen as normal and correct because one was no longer consciously aware of it anymore. It operated out of the unconscious and has generated the suffering we see on Earth today.

We need to look into our soul and perceive the reflex responses before they are suppressed by our rational consciousness. Our subconscious reflexes and reactions are set to defense and fear of enemies. The world of our movies loves images of destruction and downfall. In science fiction when extraterrestrials visit Earth, they are automatically ascribed hostile intentions, for the collective imagination of our time is hardly able to conceive of something different. The realm of fantasy, from the epic of Gilgamesh to the Brothers Grimm and to Hollywood, is a realm of danger and catastrophe. The person who has dropped out of the universal order is on his own and must try to resolve the difficulties of his life by the strength of his ego, as the universal self is no longer accessible.

When the human community is once again embedded in the great order of nature and creation, the universal human being arises as a new morphogenetic field; he is fundamentally different from the individualized ego-person. The universal human being lives in universal connectedness. He has irrevocably stepped out of the historic isolation, which he called "individualism." Also the civil servant behind the desk or the police officer controlling traffic (if these jobs still exist) will have become participants of the new human community. The universal human being has recognized its entelechial image which units us with one another and all fellow beings. It is the great image of oneness. Through the reintegration into the universal community of life, energy currents in the organism begin to operate which can heal even supposedly incurable diseases.

On this point I find the words of Master Eckhart, the great Medieval German mystic and theologian, moving. He writes…

> *All distance and alienation of the beings among one another and toward God is against God. For God lures and draws everything toward unity and commonality. And basically all beings, even the lowliest creatures strive toward togetherness, toward unity that lies in the ultimate oneness with the One.*[5]

Toward the One

All beings are interconnected in one existence and one consciousness. All beings carry the same elementary information of life in the nuclei of their cells; all carry the same basic mathematical structure in their genetic code. All beings strive for contact and unity, toward the one. In this unity a religious component is at work. "God," said the human being when he or she experienced oneness. *"Only God exists,"* declared Jacques Lusseyran when he experienced oneness at Buchenwald concentration camp, and in this he also included the guards.[6] He was able to make it as one of only thirty survivors from a group of two thousand French resistance fighters deported to the camp. *"Everything is Vasudeva,"* said Sri Aurobindo when he sat in prison awaiting a death sentence.[7] He was released. Those were not empty words, but genuine experiences of a higher level of existence, divine *unio mystica* (see Glossary). These reports also illustrate how the consciousness of oneness proffers immense protection.

People, groups, or projects that perceive themselves as part of a greater whole are under cosmic protection insofar as this greater entity is coherent with the Sacred Matrix. Should such an experience of unity happen collectively, in for example the Middle East, we would instantly have a completely new basis for the harmonious coexistence of its peoples. The conflict between Israel and Palestine would no longer be the subject of unending war, but of a common path toward the one. The (former) soldiers and guards would be profoundly changed within the fields of new peace thoughts. Fanatics full of hatred would transform into committed and approachable peace workers. This is more than just a wishful dream; it is a real possibility of our evolution – and it is probably the only viable one we have left. But first we need to straighten out our love relationships. I intentionally state this casually, almost jokingly, but its validity has become clear through many years of research. We certainly need to change a lot of things – to create ecological, spiritual, technological, and political innovations; yet above all we need a new cultural paradigm for human coexistence, especially for the love between the genders: a global correction of our notions of love, sex, and family. So far everything has failed due to flawed notions of love. So long as the structures of nuclear family, jealousy, hatred, and revenge endure in love, there will be violence and war in the world. So long as it is normal that love partners have to hide their sexual desire for others, there can be no peace in the world. These are correlations we need to understand if we want to develop practicable concepts for healing humankind and the Earth, and for establishing functioning communities. Truth in sexuality, healing in love, ending the war between the genders – there is no getting around it.

The individual belongs to community, the community is a unit within humanity, and humanity has its place in the living universe. Every person is a citizen of the universe. He is therefore subject not only to societal laws, but also to the spiritual and ethical laws of the cosmic world. These are the laws of oneness, resonance, power, and love. The universal human being is an individual that has, in his innermost core, reconnected with the universal body of life, the laws of universal life, the original field of love, and the fundamental ethics of compassion. He has decisively stepped out of the great trauma which had wedged him into the cage of psychological abandonment. This is perhaps the furthest our imagination can reach – leaving forever the desolate image of isolation and stepping into a new field of unity, power, and solidarity with all beings. *Tat tvam asi* (Thou art That – see Glossary).

A New Genetic Code for Life on Earth

Humanity needs a new informational matrix, the activation of a new genetic program for life on Earth. It is the research assignment of our time to establish such a matrix and to arrange our behavior patterns, our love relationships, our gardens, our housing, our supply systems, and our communication systems in accordance with it. Concrete utopia will be manifested through our daily work. For example, in creating a garden one would cooperate with the soil dwellers and the oft-called pests, instead of exterminating them. I would like to refer the reader to Eike Braunroth's work on establishing "Peace Gardens."[8]

Within this new matrix, all efforts will revolve around reconnecting the human world with the divine world; this is not based on conventional religious thinking, but on the most advanced contemporary knowledge and ability. I repeat again the simple thought that humankind, which is capable of developing digital weapons, will also be able to develop a new concept of life if it focuses its abilities in that direction. The worldwide enterprises of Google, Apple, Facebook, et cetera came out of the garages of Silicon Valley. Similarly, the new human world will emerge from the first communities that committedly work in this new direction. They are working not only for themselves but also according to a plan which has become ripe within the *implicate order* (see Glossary) of the universe. By activating this plan, they move the spirit body of the Earth, the noosphere, into the direction of its manifestation. The world is in an *excited state* (see Glossary) for the birth of a new era. Evolution guides the dispersed particles back to their point of convergence. Here is the new "I," the seedling of the planetary self within the consciousness of humanity as it awakes. From here life merges in a new union. The revolution of our time consists of a system change from the paradigm of separation to the paradigm of reunification within the universal family of life.

Survival Fields: Reestablishing Original Trust

We are witnessing the destruction of the world. Through the devastation of nature and the disastrous management of water, the processes of centralization and globalization, humanity has undermined the foundations for secure material existence. The material misery is so striking all over the globe that its inner aspect finds too little consideration – the aspect of psychological despair. Western societies are endangered mainly because they have lost social and psychological basis for a stable existence. Part of this basis is self-acceptance, trust, compassion, and protection. Survival will be achieved if every individual is embedded in a broader community. Happiness derives from the embedment in something greater. Partnership and family are also meant to be embedded within the higher order of a functioning community. As soon as the individual loses this embedment despair ensues. A large part of humanity currently lives in this state of despair. The fearless state of original trust was succeeded by a general disposition of caution and security. Every child comes to this world with unreserved trust, but often by the age of ten he already behaves like a small, mistrusting adult. If we have the opportunity to observe children in protected environments we immediately see what real trust looks like. It is enchanting to observe the kind of love, care, and fairness with which they approach each other. An aspect of concrete utopia becomes directly visible and so too when we see their curiosity and their high spirits, as when they somersault into water. The joy of creation – *Ananda* (see Glossary) – is undeniably a component of our genetic equipment, for it is part of the divine world. Likewise sex, love, partnership, and community are components of the Sacred Matrix when they are not distorted and destroyed through fear. In order to survive, the basis of original trust must be reestablished. By this I mean trust among human beings, trust between human and animal, and the original trust of the human being within the higher realms. **A goal of Healing Biotopes is the reestablishment of this original trust.** A key question to political and alternative groups is: do you trust one another? Trust is not only classified as psychological; it is above all a political term – the most revolutionary of all – for we need to renew the entire societal structure to bring about sustainable, systemic trust. **As soon as the individual can once again enter an atmosphere of trust, he can open up for love. Through this opening the energy of the divine field of original power is rediscovered, and thereby the era of the free human being begins.**

Humankind has been working on material science for centuries, but we do not yet have a science of love. We have started from the premise that our world is determined by physical laws, however we could also start from the premise that it is determined by laws of the soul which have something to do with love. Love is the gateway between humankind and God, the interface between personal and transpersonal worlds. From this connection an undercurrent of joy and certainty steers our behavior. If this process unfolds in the communities of the future, a collective survival field can emerge which will eventually be stronger than the deathly fields of today's global capitalism. At a certain level of maturity and intensity, these survival fields will come into high resonance with each other and with the frequencies of the Sacred Matrix. A *carrier wave* (see Glossary) will arise and spread the new informational matrix in the planetary field of life. If a prayer is spoken somewhere in this sacred network, it will become effective everywhere. The entire biosphere starts rejoicing once this resonance is reached.

Every true Healing Biotope generates a survival field. The emergent planetary community will develop from a network of such survival fields. The survival fields grow out of an enduring combination of mental and spiritual practice, technical research, and work on restoring nature and love; working with animals is included as well. The same universal energy is effective in all areas and in all those realms we can direct the currents of life toward healing. The project leaders from the individual areas are in continual communication with one another in order to align the different departments into a unified and coherent information system.

Overcoming Fascism

We are living in times of change. We are facing a planetary renewal that we did not see when we were fighting the system with anti-fascist slogans in the students' movement of the last century. Latent fascism is present everywhere; it is the cancer of humanity. It is not effective to fight fascism with ideology; this cannot change much. Once one has understood what actually happened in German fascism under Hitler, what gruesome things were done, or at least accepted, by millions of citizens, then all anti-fascist slogans and all democratic assurances fall silent, for one understands that another issue is at hand here.

Fascism is an inherent component of our current society. It develops in the subconscious of our human relationships. In the emotional substrata of a misguided civilization lie the horrible powers that led to Nazi Germany and which currently lead to very similar atrocities in many countries on Earth.

In order to overcome fascism we need a new model for our civilization that enables a fundamental renewal in the core human realms of sex, love, partnership, and community, for it is here above all that we find the psychological origins for the emergence of fascist violence. Alice Miller studied the biographies of known dictators and criminals and always arrived at the same conclusion: **when thoughts and feelings are suppressed already in childhood, the seeds for hatred and violence are sown.**[9]

Wherever the juridical and moral systems are no longer sufficient in controlling violence, the cruelty currently raging across the entire globe becomes visible. I hesitate to look into this again but the tragedy of our time demands it. On television I saw an American mother whose son, a soldier in Iraq, had been killed. She was told that he was killed by militia defending the old regime. What she did not know was that they had bound him to a car and dragged him to death (the Americans did similar things there). It is no longer only the violence of murder, but the infernal gruesomeness with which the assassination is carried out. Who are the killers, and why are they doing this? If we shed light on the biographies of the assassins we find hardly any childhoods characterized by joy and trust.

Fascism is the result of collective sexual and emotional suppression, as well as the result of a collective disenfranchisement. As Wilhelm Reich observed, the German people exploded into fascism under Hitler because they had been prohibited from expressing elementary sexual and emotional energies over centuries.[10] Looking from this perspective we realize how imperative it is that we liberate our sexual and emotional relations from all falsehood and meanness if we want to create a future without violence. In Tamera we have a research practice that we call "trauma work" or "the dissolution of inner minefields." We do this from the conviction that we need to concentrate our positive powers so that inner conflicts can no longer lead to fascist thoughts or actions. Once a community has established stable positive energy, nothing terrible can happen if two parties within it find themselves in conflict. These are powers of trust. If this process is omitted, a community will fall apart. With every failed community, a dream dies; the people involved are left bewildered and are disappointed yet again. The time we live in is full of such negative experiences. Over the last decades thousands of communities around the world have fallen apart, which is why barely anyone still wants or is able to believe in the dream of community or in the success of love.

Yet new groups, determined to cooperate with life and never again with the forces of death, are sprouting up everywhere. Creating a common basis and a goal for these groups is what the global Healing Biotopes project is all about. We are creating a morphogenetic field of peace.

Individual behavior is governed by the power of fields. Fields have more influence than private opinion. It is impossible for an individual to prevail against a forceful field. Fascism drew upon the power of the field of war, which is why it could gain such great sway over individual opinions. The peace movement has to learn to leverage the power of fields in a similar way. An individual, no matter how brave he is, will fail due to the power of the current field of war. In the case of the Ukraine, we have seen how the field of public opinion blocked every attempt to create peace. This field was driven by political and economic interests of power from the West, which shaped the general opinion in the western world and moved the rulers in Kiev to send their army into east Ukraine. They could not think it through for themselves, because they were part of a field from the very beginning.

I would now like to offer some thoughts about the significance of morphogenetic fields. We need to know this in order to understand what happened during the era of German fascism, why it could happen, and how we can prevent it from happening again.

What enabled the rise of Adolf Hitler? What powers brought almost the entire world to lie at his feet? The key to Hitler's success is rooted in the historically developed **morphogenetic field of war**. The German population had been living in a latent field of war. The whole world had been under the demonic possession of this field. Hitler and his propaganda minister Goebbels were extremely successful in activating this morphogenetic field and in so doing moved all of Germany into a highly charged atmosphere of war. Individuals who wanted to counter this development with the *Christ impulse* (see Glossary), like the Protestant theologian Dietrich Bonhoeffer, had no chance; they were assassinated.[11] In order to effectively confront fascism, new fields need to be cultivated. The morphogenetic field of war must be replaced by a morphogenetic field of peace. These two fields will not automatically be of equal strength. The morphogenetic field of war already exists; human hearts and brains have been steeped in it for many thousands of years. The morphogenetic field of peace does not yet exist; it still needs to be established. **It is the task of the new centers and their media to establish and disseminate the morphogenetic field for peace. They thereby introduce a new culture.** Once it is sufficiently developed it will be in strong resonance with the power of the Sacred Matrix, and will therefore be capable of overcoming the old field of war. The morphogenetic field of peace is comprised of more than the moralistic stance of individuals; it encompasses our relationship to nature and all fellow beings; it contains a new embedment of human society into the life of the universe. Peace among human beings, peace with all creatures, peace with the Earth.

The Foundation of the Project

After all the political, therapeutic, and spiritual stages we went through, we have returned to a basic source of humanity. Original human values such as truth, trust, love, and community are what triumphs over war and ensure survival. It is up to us to develop new ways of living that work according to these values: forms of coexistence that no longer force us to lie; communities where deceit and betrayal have no evolutionary advantage anymore; love relationships free of spite and hypocrisy. We set up "greenhouses of trust," Healing Biotopes, to foster the trustful coexistence of people with all beings. Yes, we need this new direction of evolution wherein an age-old memory will reappear to us – the primal memory of life's sacredness and the sacred alliance with all fellow inhabitants, both visible and invisible. In the 1970s our urge for this grew so strong that we needed to start.

In Germany, in the spring of 1978, with Sabine Lichtenfels, Rainer Ehrenpreis, and five other friends, I founded a research group with the question of global healing. This gave rise to a community and later to founding Tamera in southern Portugal in 1995, where the project is now based. Tamera is a research station, where approximately 160 people are currently living and working with the intention of building a first model for Terra Nova.

We have tried to find answers for the fundamental issues of human life – first to the social questions of sex, love, partnership, children, and community, and later increasingly for global problems concerning water, nutrition, and energy – in connection with our growing awareness of their interrelatedness. We have seen that the biological and technological prerequisites for a healthy human existence are linked with the psychological, sexual, ethical, and spiritual prerequisites.

It is not easy to form an enduring community with people that did not know each other previously. We faced innumerable sexual, social, pedagogic, and ethical questions, which we did not yet have answers to. In the early days there were regular misunderstandings, not least because the founders themselves were unsure as to which way to guide. The project is growing and will long continue to grow because it corresponds to an objective necessity and because it established a social basis able to withstand difficult conflicts. We are looking forward to every new person that wants to collaborate with Tamera and in the global network.

PART II
CONCRETE UTOPIA

Chapter 6: What Will Happen After the Collapse of the Globalized Systems?

A Network of New Centers

The patriarchal era began with the building of the Egyptian pyramids. With this an historic course was set in the evolution of consciousness. That which was originally recognized as eternal and sacred was distorted into an impulsive power. The pyramids, built to receive and concentrate cosmic powers, became a symbol and instrument of Earthly domination. Five thousand years have since past. This period has been characterized by the field of male, imperialist power and by the elimination of the feminine sources of life. Latest with the triumph of Rome two thousand years ago, the essential psychological features of the current era were instituted. The nineteenth and twentieth centuries were shaped by the law of capital, which quickly spread across the entire planet. This is a classic example of the effect of morphogenetic fields, unfortunately taking a catastrophic direction. All areas of life – production, energy, water, nutrition, art, morality, love, sports, et cetera – became subject to the laws of capital and humanity followed that law. Today a painting, however banal it might be, is considered to be artistically valuable when it is auctioned for ten million dollars. A business is deemed to be successful if it yields enough profit, regardless of how it is achieved. Florist companies become successful by creating flower plantations in Africa, the irrigation of which deprives native people of their groundwater. The entire planet suffered, and still suffers, from international barbarism for which nobody any longer wants to or can assume responsibility. Whoever wants to keep up must consent to the rules of this barbaric game. We are currently experiencing strange happenings in international politics; these are signs of the general decline toward dilapidation and lack of orientation. The system seems no longer capable to stand its ground. What will come next?

Put very succinctly: the old mega-systems will be replaced by decentralized, small-scale, largely self-sufficient systems, which supply humanity with the basic material necessities (water, energy, food) as well as culture, spirituality, and Eros. This movement will lead to a gradual dissolution of nation states. They will be superseded by planetary citizenship. A person's home will no longer be determined by the place of his origin, but by his position and collaboration in a grander plan. New international groups will form on all continents for the creation of Terra Nova. Young people will find the place where they can best exercise their strengths in service. The new communities will be organically interconnected through technological, political, and spiritual communication systems; together they will form the basic structure of a new global society. The upcoming era will emerge from a network of such autonomous centers; it is their task to build a morphogenetic field for the foundation of a new culture. To enable this they will collaborate within a network of global communication and information, sharing their new experiences with all who participate in them. This is how the new morphogenetic field arises as an historic process of ever-condensing information. It is the information of Terra Nova.

The new planetary community will spread rapidly as soon as the first functioning models exist. The creation of Healing Biotopes, model universities, regional cultural centers, new functioning model villages with *Water Retention Landscapes* (see Glossary), ecological neighborhoods, futuristic desert cities, global communication systems, and networks of new kinds – it is probable that these are the things we will already see around the world within the next two or three decades. The world is pregnant with the great plan of Terra Nova. As soon as this plan is recalled and implemented somewhere, a planetary impulse for its manifestation ensues. All over the world – from the Anastasia group in Russia, to the human rights groups in Europe, to the peace villages in Colombia – new centers that are aware of their interconnectedness in the birthing of the new Earth will come into being.

If this model prevails, thousands of such new living cells will evolve worldwide, for almost any terrain can be turned into fertile soil and provide humankind with sufficient nourishment. The information that humanity and nature are completely curable will sweep over the Earth with great force and ignite new sparks in human consciousness. When the dispersed elements of the great family of life are reunited, when the aforementioned groups around the world have established their networks, when love can once again enter the hearts of young revolutionaries, then the global chain reaction will be unstoppable.

The imperialistic epoch has lasted for five thousand years. Now it is breaking apart because it does not correspond with the fundamental order of life and the Earth. The more humanity accepts the fundamental order, the further our trauma will be overcome – a trauma which planted a vile historic dead-end into the heart of the human race. Profound *metanoia* (see Glossary) will occur worldwide offering orientation toward the goal of the current global transformation. It is the conversion of the human being, an anthropological revolution.

Terra Nova: An Alternative to the Colonization of Mars

NASA, along with some private institutes, is engaged in an enormous research project concerning the colonization of Mars. This is no joke. Scientists foresee that Earth could soon become uninhabitable and are seeking new possibilities for human habitation. They are thus seriously considering transforming the ice-cold planet Mars, fifty million kilometers from Earth, in such a way that humankind can live there. The utopian nature of plans such as these fascinates me, as they show what is possible today if one is technically capable. Yet these visionaries fail to see that they would simply export all of the inner social, mental, and spiritual structures that led to the devastation of Earth to another planet. How much power, how much intelligence and money is invested into this insane project! Would it not be more intelligent to put thought into new ways of living on our own planet, enabling a future that is worth living here on Earth? Would this really be more difficult than colonizing Mars? The possibilities for a humane habitation of Earth have by no means been exhausted. We are just beginning to discover them. New doors are opening in all areas of research. In science and technology, in sports, medicine, and pedagogy we are encountering revelations which only a few decades ago we would have dismissed as utter nonsense. In this context I appeal to the high-tech workers of Silicon Valley and to all visionaries of the digital world: dedicate your abilities to collaborating on the Terra Nova project. The digital world and the spiritual world are closely related; both are based on information. This is why it is possible to translate spiritual information systems, the information systems of the living world and human consciousness, into digital systems. So please, activate the information of peace and trust, digitalize the *Christ code* (see Glossary), find an information program for the noosphere in which the universal frequency of life (the *Alpha frequency* – see Glossary) is harmonized with the Christ code. Enter it into your information systems. It would be a fascinating research assignment to develop a digital pattern for the morphogenetic field of a new culture described in this book.

The Terra Nova project entails the creation of a new concept for inhabiting planet Earth by harnessing all potential inherent in a synergetic cooperation between humans and the Earth. Mars is still largely undiscovered. Is the same not also true for the Earth – its sand, its water, its creatures, and its own life? How would humanity manage water when it follows the discoveries of Viktor Schauberger? This man discovered secrets that will revolutionize our water and energy management in the near future. The last era was characterized by the exploitation of the Earth and its beings; the new era will be characterized by cooperation with its powers and creatures. I mean this literally. Cooperation with all we have hitherto fought and disregarded as "pests." Nothing was more surprising in our project's research than the cooperation with rats. They left our houses once we had established a field of genuine friendliness in relation to them; and to a great extent they complied with our proposed rules. (Whoever is wondering how something like this could work, might look into the concept of *devas*.[1]) Rats are no less members of the great family of life, to which we ourselves belong. The more we enter into this family, the more deeply we recognize the interdependence of all its beings. We will support and not destroy them. This is a paradigm of the new era: we will engage with all fellow creatures with solidarity and readiness to help.

Chapter 7: The Inner Operator

Satprem, a student of Sri Aurobindo, tells a wonderful story about his own salvation. It shows how an assassination is prevented through the intervention of higher consciousness. One morning Satprem was at the edge of a canyon, the place he used to sit for his morning meditation. Suddenly three men who were assigned to kill him appeared. He did not react but observed the whole spectacle as if from the outside. Thereupon the hand that went to swing at him dropped and the assassins ran away. They were no longer capable of carrying out the murder.[1] The impulses to violence were extinguished, as Satprem gave no resonance to them, reacting without fear or hatred. The "inner operator" had intervened and transformed the scene. Satprem stood there without the fear he would normally have had. Violence dissipates if we do not give resonance to it through fear or counter-violence, which is why the assassins' murderous intentions suddenly receded. No longer able to carry out their assignment, they simply fled.

This story reminds us of the training of the Samurai who is only capable of victory once he is able to not react to the blows of his opponents with fear or hatred. Here we encounter a basic rule of committed peace work: never react to an opponent with fear or hatred. Furthermore, never react to the general world situation with fear or hatred. With every occurrence of fear or hatred we lose power. A principle of successful peace and healing work consists of maintaining an inner state permanently free of fear and hatred. For this we need familiarity with higher consciousness.

Lao Tsu writes in the *Tao Te Ching*...

> *He who is skillful in managing the life entrusted to him for a time travels on the land without having to shun rhinoceros or tiger, and enters a host without having to avoid buff coat or sharp weapon. The rhinoceros finds no place in him into which to thrust its horn, nor the tiger a place in which to fix its claws, nor the weapon a place to admit its point. And for what reason? Because there is in him no place of death.*[2]

What Lao Tsu claims here is utterly incredible. He says that there is an inner guidance that protects us from calamity. When we are holding the right frequency nothing will harm us. He who plunges down a waterfall and stays connected to his *hara* (see Glossary) will arrive at the bottom safely. This suggests that there is a frequency in which survival is guaranteed. Does it really exist?

I know it from my own experience. There is an inner operator, which in critical situations reminds us of a deeper knowledge or takes over the steering wheel when we are unable to find the corrective maneuver. Everyone has a so-called "guardian angel." We can understand this as an aspect of our consciousness, which offers advice or drives action toward healing or salvation. The potentialities inherent within us seem to be unlimited. It is as if each of us has a kind of super-brain, which bestows upon us faculties far beyond our usual capabilities. Parapsychologists speak of *psi* abilities (see Glossary) in this context. No matter how we explain it, these abilities originate from a meta-world; a more comprehensive understanding would require thorough study of the functions and principles operative in the spiritual world. K.O. Schmidt, an expert in spiritual healing writes…

> *There is an omnipresent, omniscient, and omnipotent power within me. It knows what serves my well-being and how to achieve it. Originating in the divine, it becomes effective in my being, in my body, and even beyond in my environment, arranging and harmonizing, guiding, helping, and healing to the degree I remain open and receptive to its instruction and help.*[3]

Are we really able to grasp the meaning of this statement?

This power exists objectively; it is the highest organ of human consciousness. With lightning speed, it sends saving impulses when we are in a hopeless situation. With lightning speed, Satprem could switch his consciousness in the face of assassins and they therefore could not harm him. With lightning speed, a higher power took over my steering wheel when my car spun out on an icy patch in the Harz Mountains and hurtled into oncoming traffic. We can give various names to this power. The "operator," the "higher self," the "super-brain," the "*supramental*" (see Glossary), or simply "God." What matters in this context is the acknowledgement of this power and to offer it much greater influence in our lives than we have given it so far. The presence and operative logic of this higher power should be studied in the universities of the new Earth.

Sri Aurobindo, the famous Indian yoga philosopher, worked on the revolutionary side in the Indian struggle for independence from the British and was about to be sentenced to death, alongside his brother.

Briefly before the trial, Vasudeva (the Indian God) appeared to him and said...

> *Remember never to fear, never to hesitate. Remember that it is I who am doing this, not you nor any other. Therefore whatever clouds may come, whatever dangers and sufferings, whatever difficulties, whatever impossibilities, there is nothing impossible, nothing difficult. It is I who am doing this.*[4]

Aurobindo was set free. His brother who had committed the same "crime" was executed.

Here we gain a first insight as to what this inner power could be. It refers to itself as "I" – it speaks about itself in the first person; it calls itself God. God (Vasudeva) tells the human being: I am this power, not you nor any other. But as this power is supposedly within the human being, as K.O. Schmidt claims, we need to recognize – in addition to the usual self – a higher self, which guides us as far as we are open to it. We are thus presented with a remarkable hypothesis which could characterize our existence in the approaching era: we "small" beings carry within ourselves the grand entity, that which we have formerly elevated above all things and called God. We carry within ourselves the abilities and potentials, which we had previously projected on an external creator! This mysterious subject of the world – the divine "I" – is ultimately us, once we have connected with our higher self. This could be the next steps on our journey through evolution, the inner journey from the egoic "I" to the universal or divine "I," from private thinking to universal consciousness, from individual strength to universal force. The further the human being progresses on this journey, the more power he will gain over himself, his emotions, and his habits. He is on the way to regaining lost power.

It is the way of healing. It is the message of the new time. It is the big promise behind the small sentence: *"let go and let God."* Whosoever is under such guidance need no longer worry, *"for it is not you who speaks, but it is the Holy Spirit."*[5] There is something carrying us when we cannot bring ourselves further, an intelligence beyond our own, a knowing that enters when we open the appropriate channels, as if suddenly the full hundred percent of our brain were activated (as opposed to the estimated ten percent of our usual usage.) Here a course in the spiritual evolution of humankind is revealed, **the handing over of the direction of our lives to a higher intelligence, which is** ultimately our "own." The meaning and goal of humanity's current transformation lies in this surrendering.

Chapter 8: The Sacred Matrix

How is it that there has been a universal symbolic language which has repeated in all places throughout humanity's cultural history? Why is it that the same basic mathematic pattern occurs in the genetic code and in the I Ching?[1] Why have architects over the centuries attempted to design buildings according to *sacred geometry* (see Glossary)? It is because there is a pattern in the universe that shines through all that exists. The phenomenon of the analogy between the I Ching and the genetic code is a wonderful illustration of this. Both are expressions of a kind of "world formula" – the I Ching from the realm of mystery knowledge and the genetic code from the realm of molecular biology. The structures of both are mathematically almost identical; it is the same fundamental cosmic pattern in two disciplines that could not be more different!

The Sacred Matrix is the cosmic pattern, the morphogenetic field of the universe, which forms the basis for the organization of life. It steers the information and energies necessary for the evolution and maintenance of life. When the individual connects with this guidance, channels for healing open up. When humanity orients its Earthly existence, its social structures, energy systems, water and food systems in accordance with the Sacred Matrix, channels for global healing powers open up. The principle of global healing relies on the congruence of our actions with the direction of energy and order inherent in the Sacred Matrix. This congruence is encoded in the structure of creation, for the Sacred Matrix is also inscribed in the genetic pattern of the human being, in the molecular structure of our DNA. It operates in our intrapersonal life as an *original matrix* (see Glossary) of love, and it operates our interpersonal lives as an original matrix of community. Healing occurs by activating the original matrix.

The original matrix of human community demands from us a new way of coexisting with the other members in the great family of life. It has to be a new form of "communism" or "socialism." Historically these terms have been derided but their content is just beginning to gain meaning. This new socialism encompasses everything that belongs to the original matrix of community: the liberation of sexuality, the cooperation with nature, and the communication with cosmic entities. It is a task of our time to translate this original matrix into a new political language and to find forms of governance to coordinate the new cells of the global community without violence.

There is a genetic pattern steering our behavior. Through the mores of human society some aspects of this pattern (i.e. certain segments of the DNA) were activated and other aspects deactivated. The result is the collective orientation of a society toward a particular matrix of information. The peace workers of our time have the task to change this matrix and to develop information that is oriented toward the precepts of the Sacred Matrix. This shall not only happen symbolically (as in sacred geometry) but concretely and dynamically in the establishment of new societal systems. **As soon as the new systems are compatible with the Sacred Matrix they will prevail worldwide, for all people are connected to this matrix.**

Chapter 9: The Power of Christ

Here we come to a difficult issue. The title of this chapter sits uneasily in the current zeitgeist. I want to describe something that takes place every time that two or more people are in a state of coherence or synergy with each other. This situation creates an opening through which a healing power enters that dissolves old hostilities and fears. When I witness this effect I cannot think of other words; I call it the "power of Christ." In our healing work we experienced the disappearance of digestive disorders, abdominal inflammations and acute eczemas when this power enters. There are many such reports of extraordinary healings; this opening can even restore sight to blind people. In our pilgrimages in Colombia and Israel-Palestine we saw people, formerly hostile to each other, lying in each other's embrace once they were taken by this power. It is a universal force that is clearly beyond any cultural or religious tradition and which becomes operative everywhere that an opening occurs.

In today's struggle between ideology and emotions there is a problem that always crops up and about which I have often been challenged. Talking about Christ with the revolutionary vanguard pushes everyone's buttons. Too much killing and lying has been carried out, too much suffering inflicted, in the name of Christ. I am aware how problematic it is today to use this kind of vocabulary given that it has such vile historic connotations. Were not the major religions of East and West used to subjugate people that they would serve the purposes of the ruling powers? Did not the most diabolical things happen in the name of the Lord, in the name of Yehova and in the name of Allah? Why would we not renounce religion once and for all and solve our problems in more sober and humane ways? In 1968 I was a spokesman of the Marxist movement and was an ardent proponent of the statement, *"religion is the opiate of the masses"*[1] because religion **was** an opiate for the people.

I use the term "the power of Christ" nevertheless. In doing so I do not refer to a particular religion but to a universal phenomenon. In the current global situation we no longer need religious evangelism but to explore the interconnectedness of the spiritual realm from which we all come. There are discoveries of a spiritual cosmology which challenge us to use certain terms even when they have been abused and distorted for centuries. Christ is an archetype within the collective human soul, deeply inscribed into our genetic and psychological matrix. We all know and love this image even if we reject it.

The divine figure manifests within human beings through our connection with the divine world. All religious and spiritual traditions attest to this, calling it variously "Atman," "Buddha," "Shekinah," "Christ," or the "Higher Self." When I speak of the *Christ nature* (see Glossary) in this chapter I have chosen, from all the historical variations, the one that I feel to be closest to the spirit of love. Christ is the epitome of love. Whoever finds the word Christ too masculine can replace it with the "Marian nature" because this is the feminine aspect of the cosmic Christ figure.

All authentic religions revolved around a shift in the perception and understanding of the self, a shift of the inner *assemblage point* (see Glossary) from a separated, ego identity to a divine identity – the "higher self." This is the divine consciousness as it resides in individual human beings or as Teilhard de Chardin said, *"the inner station of God."*[2] Different impulses and information enter into our system when we are at this point. Our brains begin to function differently, releasing new "messengers," neuropeptides, and our nuclei produce new proteins. Another hologram of life comes into being.

I venture right into a utopian direction when I say that the human of the future is a "Christ-being." This is how it was meant to be; this is our *entelechy* (see Glossary). Today, when we speak of peace, healing and love, we are walking in this direction. In the words of Ernst Bloch this is the *"consciousness of our advent."*[3] We live in a state of "utopian latency"[4] and activate this latent utopia when we engage, in the name of a new Earth, with the reality of our human nature beyond all religions.

One could also describe our Christ nature as the imprint of the Sacred Matrix within the human genetic system. By consciously bringing this pattern to the surface we enter a new stage in humanity's erotic, social and political evolution. We access divine powers. This activation and opening takes place in encounters filled with trust when human beings recognize each other. The promises of love and happiness, made by the old religions, find their fulfillment in relations between people here on Earth. The Kingdom of God is no longer a matter of religious belief but of creating the new social structures of human community. As soon as the Christ nature within the participants of communities is activated, a morphogenetic wave could be triggered that draws us all in for it touches something that is the same within everyone.

Today we are still in the storm of an historic era of war in which the behavior of mankind has strayed far from its Christ nature. People like Jesus, Mani, and thousands of others who remained faithful to their Christ consciousness were overpowered by the system. Single human beings confronting an organized apparatus of power did not stand a chance. If the global peace workers of our time want to reach their goal they need to establish a new "system" wherein the Christ power is anchored in the social and ecological order of the communities. It is not the power of individuals but a complex combination of people, animals, waters and natural powers that establishes a force, coherent with the Sacred Matrix that is capable of offering evolution a new direction.

Christ is a futurological figure that is inherent to us as the butterfly is to the caterpillar. The transformations that the caterpillar needs to undergo in order to manifest as the butterfly can be seen as analogous to the transformations which humankind today needs to undergo in order to realize the goal of its entelechy. In the old power systems of state and religion this goal was barely visible but it has shone through time and again throughout human history. Plato's theory of forms refers to the *Agathon* (see Glossary), the absolute goodness.[5] This idea could not have arisen if the Agathon did not exist as a latent reality within humanity. It is not only in the thoughts of gifted philosophers that we find testimony to the existence of the Christ power; we find it also amidst the horrors of war. The reports by Jacques Lusseyran of his experiences in Buchenwald offer moving insights into the Christ nature of the erstwhile criminals who were his fellow prisoners. I have also been personally struck by the Christ nature in those who have helped me in times of severe illness.

As we succeed in freeing primordial images of love from false morality and sentimentality the participants within the new communities will recognize the grand goal to which we are walking. The history of the Tamera project is the story of journey such as this; it has just begun. All of the groups and projects collaborating in the great plan will undergo a process of transformation akin to that of the caterpillar. While the sentence, *"God is love"*[6] has lost its meaning for quite a while, perhaps today we can understand it anew. To the extent that the Christ nature is manifested in human relationships, a morphogenetic field of love comes into being and thereby begins a historic cultural shift. Terra Nova is a love affair.

Chapter 10: Ananda

Alongside the tormented world there exists another – the world of joy, of Ananda. Its laws should form the basis for the new culture. Ananda is what Indian yogis understand as the original state of existence. Ananda means something like primordial joy. Primordial joy is an integral part of life so long as its freedom is not violated. Playing dogs and cats are full of Ananda. We are touched by their playfulness, for we instinctively recognize what they are doing. We human beings also carry the "Ananda gene" within us and the plant world is full of it too. Ananda is the source of life; it is this that we see at work in the restoration of degraded ecosystems. I find it moving to see how quickly a parched landscape regenerates as soon as water retention basins are introduced. In a short time an eroded, arid zone transforms into a fecund biotope abundant in diverse flora and fauna. The work of the Permaculture specialist Sepp Holzer[1] and Tamera's Water Retention Landscape are good examples of this. One has to see it to believe it. It is as if the program for joy is always present in nature and can manifest immediately once people re-establish the necessary conditions. Nature's original matrix only waits to be understood and newly awakened by humanity. The same applies to our contact with animals. Animals meet people with unreserved joy when they recognize they no longer need to fear them. In Tamera we have often experienced the growing trust of animals. Turtles in our lakes swim toward us, until they brush up against us. Water snakes weave around our legs; one rested on a woman's belly. Pigs jump with joy when we approach them; one once turned a perfect pirouette. Eagles and vultures circle above us. We know of enchanting photos which capture trust between animals and human beings – a zoo keeper embraced by lions and a baby stroking the head of an enormous Python. One can sense the mutual joy of living beings as they discover each other. Could this world not be paradise? After eons of fear and separation everything yearns for contact and reunion. The world stirs from ossification and begins to dance with joy like the Namibian antelopes at the coming of the first rain after a long dry spell. This is the pure bliss of creation. This is the concrete utopia in its full abundance. This is Terra Nova.

If we turn from this vantage point and fleetingly look at the everyday happenings in slaughterhouses, fur farms, and animal laboratories, we observe them almost like retrospective history. The contrast could not be more blatant. Each of us faces an unavoidable decision: For how long are we willing to participate, directly or indirectly, in such heinousness? Complicity is an ethical and political concern. The establishment of autonomous supply systems as part of Terra Nova is imperative on ethical ground alone, as they free us from the dependency on a ruthless system of production and consumption. We cannot step fully into cooperation with the divine world so long as we torment or neglect its creatures for all are members of the same family of life. The reestablishment of this primordial union is a prerequisite for a future without fear. The sacred alliance of all that lives wants to reunite. We see that this could be; we clearly see a world without fear. No animal will be afraid of human beings when human beings no longer fear animals and so cease to torment them. No human being will fear another when there is no longer cause for hatred and violence. We are in the sacred alliance with all beings; this is how it is written in the plan of creation; and in case this was not yet the plan of the old world, then it is the plan of the new world that we want to bring to life in the next step of evolution. The old, deeply ingrained fear will be replaced by a joy of life; a primordial, unconditional joy for **life is primordial joy**. We see this in every cat, every dog, every child.

Life is primordial joy; we had almost forgotten. Nature's celebration is attended by the celebration of love. The Holy Grail is now no longer found in dreary forests, but in all creatures' bliss of existence. When our dismay at the world situation wants to overwhelm us, we should remember that Ananda is a more meaningful basis for healing the world.

Chapter 11: The Holy Land

It is a celebration to build the new Earth in alliance with all fellow beings. When people are united in such celebration, the Holy Land arises. Jesus' dream of the coming of the "kingdom" finds fulfillment and the "heavenly Jerusalem" comes down to Earth. We arrive in the Promised Land "Canaan," but this land is not located by the Jordan River; it is everywhere that human beings resurrect it. This requires no peoples to be expelled and no biotope to be destroyed. We know the sacred myths about the "Holy Land" and the "heavenly kingdom on Earth." The idea of transforming an Earthly kingdom into a kingdom of God and vice versa arose early in patriarchal history. The Egyptian pyramids established the cosmologic connection between the human and divine worlds; the Pharaoh Akhenaten founded the sun-city Amarna to bring the divine world to Earth.[1] Yet these attempts failed because the original enlightenment, which might well have been authentic, deteriorated into an ecstasy of imperialistic power. They lacked the transformative power of love.

Two thousand years ago, Jesus of Nazareth demonstrated how our lives on Earth could be connected to the divine world through love. To this day Jesus is a guiding figure for many people, showing how life is actually meant to be. In attempting to continue his path, while incorporating certain necessary societal conditions, we are in a sense his successors. Since Jesus' time many attempts have been made to fuse the divine and human kingdoms. From Jerusalem to Brasilia people have tried to develop architecture in accordance with the proportions of sacred geometry; the wind is blowing in this direction through many disciplines. However in all the attempts to bring God to Earth, Eros was forgotten. I have described in *The Sacred Matrix* how all social utopias to date have excluded "issue number one."[2] It is inconceivable that humanity has undertaken so much spiritual development in search of God, and in almost all attempts the core issue of our lives has remained neglected. This is a scorching issue on which we have all burnt our fingers. An issue that throughout history became so terribly linked to jealousy, revenge, and bloodshed that no one wanted to take it on again. But without solving humanity's sexual issue, without redeeming this wonderful promise for the meeting of the genders in a positive, nonviolent way, there will be no free world.

The Holy Land is not bound to any religion; it arises everywhere people see and realize this great vision. It will be a shining carpet woven through all countries, gradually encompassing the globe. We are working on a basis of life shared by all inhabitants of this planet. This should reenter our consciousness: the Healing Biotopes and new communities originate from a global movement and ethics wished for and supported by all citizens of our planet. **This movement is not brought forth by the egos of small groups, but by the global self of our planet.** We human beings are part of the world. We have injured the world and now want to heal it in accordance with its inherent nature. The Holy Land is the testament of the twenty-first century and applies to all peoples of the Earth. All of life is meant to be healed; this is the message.

"If you will it, it is no fairytale!" Theodor Herzl called out to his Jewish friends when he wanted to make the vision of a new Israeli nation accessible to them.[3] But he ignored the Palestinians already living there and he did not yet know the inner sexual, social, and ecological conditions for a humane world. *"If you will it, it is no fairytale"* – this is how we can once again say it if we refer to a reunited humanity that in deep cooperation with the powers of creation brings paradise to Earth as it was laid out in the entelechial program of all beings.

The highest and, for the time being, last conclusion from our current journey through all the promises of science and religion is that we will enter into a world where we love and care for our surrounding, as we recognize the divine presence in it. We will see every plant as a symbol of the higher world once the secret within it has been revealed to us. One's life will change once one has **really** seen a blossom.

Chapter 12: Water, Food, and Energy are Freely Available to Humankind

Nature produces in abundance that which humanity needs – oxygen, water, and nutrition. All people and animals of the Earth could be fed if the mechanisms of our global economy would orient in relation to the law of nature and not the law of capital. Nature's original matrix only waits to be understood and awakened anew by humankind.

The Earth is being destroyed by the political and economic apparatus of global capitalism, and through the struggles over water, food, and energy in particular. Entire regions are being devastated and robbed of their natural resources for the production of energy, foodstuffs, and other consumer goods. When we look into the fate of the innumerable beings that fall victim to the machinery of globalization we recognize the absolute necessity of new concepts for autonomy that enable the world's population to meet their material needs independent of cartels and other power syndicates. **Decentralized autonomy, providing the greatest possible self-sufficiency, is a prerequisite for the development of a nonviolent civilization.** An energy strategy that requires storage reservoirs cannot exist in accordance with the higher laws of creation. What happens to the people living in the places in which multinational corporations plan to mine resources? What happens to the animals and the whole subtle fabric of nature fulfilling its tasks within the great organism of life? Can we look into the millions of caves, niches, nests, and micro-biotopes where animals had their homes, which are now mercilessly being flooded, centimeter-by-centimeter? This is symbolic of the unstoppable machine of extermination tearing over the globe today. What happened to the wildlife in Portugal when the Alqueva Dam was built? What is now happening in Brazil as a consequence of the Belo Monte hydropower project, where more than forty thousand native people are being driven out of their homes? What does this do to the spirit of nature and to the collective human psyche? It is intolerable how profit-driven projects such as these are pushed through by bribery, intrigue, and intentional misinformation.

We need neither storage reservoirs, nuclear power plants, nor other megaprojects to secure the supply of energy and food, for nature provides abundantly. Once the technologies developed by people such as Viktor Schauberger, Sepp Holzer, Masanobu Fukuoka, Nikola Tesla, and Juergen Kleinwaechter become widespread, there will no longer be scarcity. Agricultural projects in China and Africa have shown how quickly nature is able to regenerate as soon as it is no longer hindered by flawed management strategies. The work of John D. Liu, the filmmaker who documents the restoration of large-scale degraded eco-systems, offers an insight into the possibilities of greening deserts. Given financial support, the techniques he features could be applied worldwide. He has shown how a huge deserted area in China – the Loess Plateau – was regenerated with only simple technology.[1] He shows similar examples of nature restoration in Ethiopia, Rwanda, and other countries. Such models illustrate humanity's potential when it is no longer blocked by corporations and their political advocates.

Rajendra Singh, also known as "Water Gandhi," has greened more than 8,600 square kilometers of desert in Rajasthan, India over the course of twenty-five years, using traditional "johads" (check dams). Using simple techniques, village communities have built a retention landscape that is replenishing the aquifers. Today tens of thousands of people are able to sustain themselves from this land and are no longer forced to migrate to cities. Five rivers have been restored and now flow throughout the year and the rain has returned. To protect nature from exploitation in the future and to keep the water in the hands of the people they have founded a "river parliament."[2]

There are a significant number of similarly effective projects worldwide, but many operate in relative isolation. They need an international alliance to enable the growth of a global field for a new Earth. Healing nature, regional self-sufficiency, and international collaboration are basic conditions for ending world hunger. Each new center within the alliance should run an office for international exchange and communication.

Around the world many further developments in decentralizing water and energy supplies are underway. Many of them do not make it to production because they do not comply with contemporary policies and are therefore not funded. This is the case for research into "free energy" and the work of the engineer and inventor Juergen Kleinwaechter on new ways of utilizing solar energy and the creation of energy-autonomous communities. "Solar Village" is the name he gives the system that is to be installed in Tamera.

No child will starve once a free humanity begins using the tools already available to us. Food grows everywhere people sow seeds. All peoples of the Earth must quickly and unconditionally have their right to self-sufficiency restored to them. It is clear that the aforementioned new autonomous centers will conflict with the interests of the "other side." The "New World Order" instigated by the forces of global capitalism cannot tolerate regional self-sufficiency. But this "other side" consists only of human beings and the system they are serving is unlikely to endure much longer. We hope for opportunities to collaborate. The power struggle between the forces of life and the forces of profit must, as far as is possible, be transformed into a new model of cooperation. It has to become possible, for the old types of revolutionary struggle are no longer valid. There will be no "last holy battle." The peace movement should develop an intelligent concept for collaboration with those parts of the capitalist empire that have recognized its economic and humanitarian insanity. We should not be too fast to deride these thoughts as naïve. They are not naïve, for even now respected representatives of the current system are coming to Tamera to explore the potential for collaboration. They see that their methods in, for example water management, will not work for much longer. Once the gate for the universal concept of life is opened, our possibilities are unlimited.

Chapter 13: The Reality of the Utopian Goal

Terra Nova is the dream of a new humanity on a healed Earth. Clean rivers, blossoming meadows, fragrant forests, and a unified humankind in creative contact with all fellow beings. This dream is no longer mere wishful thinking, for it is contained as a real possibility within the existing world. Once we stop polluting them, rivers purify themselves. All living things carry an intended direction, an entelechy, an intrinsic goal. The future is inscribed within life. The concrete utopia resides as an image in every being, as the goal of its development, just as the image of the oak tree is inherent in the acorn. We are all on the way toward the realization of a goal that is encoded within us, a perfection which we have not yet attained. This "not yet" does not connote a state of deficiency, but an internal motor of life. Ernst Bloch refers in Latin to the great "nondum,"[1] the "not yet" of history, the developmental goal built into life as "utopian latency."[2] As the dream of the tree is in its seed, the dream of Terra Nova is the latent utopia of humanity, the great "nondum," a concealed but real possibility. As Jesus declared to his followers, *"behold, the kingdom of God is in your midst,"*[3] we can today say, "behold, Terra Nova is in your midst." For those with a preference for scientific formulations we might describe Terra Nova as the hologram ready to be recalled from the implicate order and to be downloaded with the appropriate frequencies. The manifestation of this utopia depends on the information we enter into the global body of life. With every action, every word, and every thought we activate or block the historic process, activate the promised utopia or its opposite.

The future lies in every cell. The famous caterpillar transforms into the famous butterfly. This is the reality of concrete utopia. The butterfly is the latent utopia within the caterpillar. The caterpillar knows nothing of it and yet within it lives the matrix of its future existence, the information of the butterfly. Could we not draw an analogy with humanity? Might information about our entelechy that has not yet been brought to life exist also in the human being? When we speak of the "higher self" or the "inner Christ," could this not refer to the true utopia of the human being we are walking toward?

While she was in a trance state I asked my partner Sabine Lichtenfels what is to be done after the catastrophes in Fukushima, Oslo, London, and other places. She answered...

*Despite what is happening in the world, you need to see
the intact reality, for the sane always exists at the same
time. The more you open up for its frequencies, the further
it can radiate and effect miracles.*[4]

The intact reality always exists. It is realized when it is seen and
activated by us. Utopia can be realized when it is recognized and
desired by the first human beings. **The potential of global healing has
to be seen and wanted. In every being, however traumatized it may
be, lies an intact and sacred original matrix that becomes effective
immediately once it is seen, addressed, and activated.** These are
tenets that will spare us much suffering when they are properly applied
to our lives.

Behind every disease is an intact matrix that begins to manifest in
the moment it is seen. What manifests in the world depends on our
perceptions and thoughts. Inherent healing powers remain operative
even when medical science no longer sees a chance. Lusseyran
survived when according to medical science he should certainly have
died (see Chapter 17).[5] **The more we succeed in establishing a
societal order – a social, sexual, ecological, and political order –
compatible with the higher order of life (the Sacred Matrix) the
more healing powers we attract and the more our longing for
utopia can find fulfillment.**

Over the ages great minds in the East, as in the West, knew that
human evolution is striving toward a most profound spiritual goal that
consists of the complete reunification of the human being with its
divine origin. Today we are still entangled in mental attachments that
we will abandon tomorrow. Attachments to a body one can touch and
to the person one can refer to. With reference to the aforementioned
image, we are analogous to the caterpillar, and thereby "identified"
with our current state of being. If we were to tell a caterpillar that it
would become a butterfly, it would denounce us as crazy and withdraw
from further debate. The same thing happens with people. Today, if one
tells somebody something about the divine nature programmed within
him, one risks suspicion of belonging to a cult or being committed to a
psychiatric ward. This is why it becomes increasingly important to find
a clear scientific language that every thinking human being can
understand. We know that we are only at the beginning of our mental
and spiritual development and that the Christ nature is contained within
all of us, waiting to be recognized and recalled so that we can realize a
concrete utopia.

The Invisible Substance

I hold an apple in my hand. Who created it? The superpower that created this apple is also able to end global war. We ourselves have emerged from this superpower and carry it within ourselves. We will learn to make use of it and thereby create a spiritual power field that changes the world as an "invisible substance." This is one of the tasks for the coming era. It is part of the coming teaching in which we will participate both as teachers and students.

In the Upanishads, one of humanity's most ancient books of wisdom, this invisible substance is the originally creative puissance in the core of the fig tree's fruit, from which the tree grew and every else also came to being. The originally creative puissance is the basic essence of the world; it is identical to Atman, the self of all beings. According to this, there is an inner essence that is the same in all beings! The invisible essence is at the root of our assertion that all beings are connected in one existence and one consciousness.

Reality is not a finished arrangement of matter, but a manifestation of invisible energy and information fields, a manifestation of consciousness, of thoughts and pictures. Within the world's fabric, consciousness and material reality are constantly interacting. Through the power of our thoughts, we are continually involved in creation. With a strong vision, we change reality. To consciousness, nothing is impossible, for "belief can move mountains." The invisible substance of our thinking is what moves the world. Our thoughts are made of the same substance as the world. This is what we want to bring into coherence so that it gives birth to a powerful new field.

The invisible substance surrounds us permanently in form of radiation and frequencies of all kinds. When I switch on the radio I receive these frequencies as music. The world is full of frequencies everywhere; the invisible substance is everywhere. There are frequencies that can be received and transformed with technological devices such as radios and television sets. There are spiritual frequencies that we receive consciously or unconsciously. It is easy to conceive that in all areas – the biological, psychological, technical, and spiritual – the invisible substance is connected. If we learn to activate the invisible substance of Terra Nova in all areas, a great manifestation power arises in the body of life – similar to how the tree emerges from the invisible substance in the seed.

Terra Nova is the image of an intact Earth. This image is not the invention of this author but a new objective possibility for life on Earth. This possibility has not yet manifested, but exists within the *holographic fabric of the world* (see Glossary) at any point. If we could see the invisible world of information and thoughts we would look into a luminous universe. It is similar to the astronomers' photos from outer space; where physicists formerly believed there to be empty space, we now begin to recognize networks of light and immaterial structures. The visible world originated from invisible energy and information. The creative potential of humanity is dependent on which information systems we activate. It is without doubt possible to create a human society from which the impulses of violence are deleted, where jealousy is no longer associated with love, and conflicts are never again addressed by war. It is possible that in the emotional system of future humanity there exists no violent inclinations because no information would be activated that could trigger them. In this way, our old fear-based life scripts can die off because they are no longer confirmed by true danger. Thus life will be free of fear. In the state of real fearlessness we experience many new things, for our interpretation of our experiences changes. We will no longer react according to projections of fear and hostility, but in accordance with our higher self. This is the beginning of a fundamental program change in the invisible substance.

We find ourselves in collective transformation. We have gone through the era of ego and now enter a new growth in consciousness. We are working on implementing a new morphogenetic field for our future on Earth. This morphogenetic field is meant to guide the inner development of humanity through the invisible substance. I repeat a maxim I used earlier: "There is the world that we create and there is the world that has created us. These two worlds must come together. That is the goal of the journey."

Chapter 14: Powers of Manifestation

To date there have been two principle modes of manifestation: magic and technology. We will come to know new systems in which magic and technology are connected. To be able to deal, both on the inner and the outer, with the tasks to come, we need to augment our material capabilities with spiritual ones. We need in particular to discover, experience, and describe the metaphysical anew. This is the power of vision, concentration, and prayer. We need a locus for this in the new centers, that which we call the "Political Ashram" in Tamera. Here, students learn how the spiritual powers of the Sacred Matrix influence the material world, and how we are therefore able to change the world through the use of spiritual powers. These powers are discovered and activated through study, prayer, and art; by visualizing the aspired goals and by increasing one's physical prowess through mental and spiritual exercises. Eugen Herrigel's book, *Zen in the Art of Archery,* delivers wonderful material for these new studies.[1] Proficiency in these practices requires work; it's not that we are expected to be competent from the outset, just that we should know that this potential is, in principle, carried within all human beings, just as dry wood contains the potential for heat and light. We need to examine this analogy thoroughly. Behind the visible world is a parallel world of undreamt possibilities. A school of a new kind is arising here to newly adjust us human beings in the thicket of the multiverse. Humanity needs to reconnect with the power that is stronger than all violence. It is the "immanent God" that guides us when we take on this work. While it may seem strange to use religious terminology here after so many centuries of religious abuse, I am not returning to outmoded belief systems. I am referring to a meta-world, toward a new continent that lies beyond old religious and scientific notions. The more the peace movement draws on this power the more certain will be its success.

Vision and Reality

We encounter new correlations between the spiritual and material worlds. The outgoing worldview was materially oriented; the incoming one will be spiritually oriented. This paradigm shift has significant consequences for our interpersonal behavior. If we form in our mind a positive image of a love partner, a business partner, or even an enemy, and if we are able to hold this image firmly and calmly, it will emerge instantly in the cellular system of the other person. He will unconsciously adapt in the direction of this "ideal" image. It is as if I would imagine writing something in my mind and it subsequently appears on a computer screen. The cyber world deals with such processes of transference all the time (see Chapter 30). The further our inquiring human consciousness advances, the more fascinating will be the possibilities that present themselves. If the mental and spiritual image we configure of another person is compatible with the potential of his genes and entelechy, it starts operating in the organism of this human being the very moment we form this picture. We are working on reformulating ancient mystery knowledge. In order to gain this knowledge one must understand the holographic and spiritual structures of reality. The power that creates the ideal image of the other within us is the same power that causes the corresponding cellular movement within him. We can extrapolate further: the power that creates the ideal image of a community is the same power that initiates the corresponding changes in the community. The power generating a vision is identical to the power that will manifest it. This is not "my" power, but that of the spiritual meta-world.

Again and again we hear of distance healing, as it is performed for example by the American "dream healer" Adam McLeod. It is based on the same principle of transmitting a mental image or thought into a material system. This could be applied to large-scale conflicts, in service of, for example, the reconciliation of peace workers and the paramilitary in Colombia, or among Israelis and Palestinians, over questions of water supply. It always works when our vision grasps that which already exists as a latent possibility.

The present transformation of human consciousness leads us to areas of research that we would have hitherto branded as occult or mysterious. We recognize that the material world is in fact generated and guided by mental and spiritual powers. It is logical that we would then engage these capacities with increasing intensity when we are focused on the effective transformation of the material world. Although the authority required to carry out the tasks which await us originates in the meta-world, that authority is no longer beyond us, but within us. It is the immanent God generating both vision and manifestation.

The Principle of Spiritual Magnetism

I begin with the beautiful words of Dhyani Ywahoo...

With the conscious decision to live in a sacred manner, we attract the understanding, the teachings, and information that will help us to unfold our gifts for the benefit of all.[2]

With the making of every conscious decision a "spiritual magnetic field" is generated, which attracts that which is needed for its realization. We can call this the principle of spiritual attraction. The success of a project depends largely on the precision of its underlying plan, the image of the goal, the spiritual scaffolding. Many groups have failed simply due to absence of an intelligent spiritual concept or an inner vision for their project. Iron particles move by themselves to their correct position in the magnetic field. This astonishing phenomenon can to a certain extent be translated to the social realm. If the spiritual blueprint is powerful it works like an attractor, drawing toward it all things necessary for its manifestation. This happens "by itself"! People take the necessary actions by themselves when they are united within the spirit of a potent plan. If the plan is coherent with the Sacred Matrix, they will be assisted by additional energies entering due to resonance with the cosmic order. The common work proceeds according to the plan's dynamic direction. The plan leads the group; the spiritual blueprint is the boss. We need neither supervising authorities nor social pressure. The only difficulty lies in constructing the spiritual blueprint and conveying it to the community. The more extensive and complex a plan is, the more difficult it becomes to communicate convincingly. The global Healing Biotopes plan is exceptionally complex; uniting a community of over one hundred people on the basis of this plan is consequently challenging. I hope that we will reach our goal and yet the Healing Biotopes plan will remain valid and necessary even in the event of Tamera not entirely fulfilling it.

The "By-Itself" Principle

The universal order of life operates according to a logic that differs fundamentally from the mechanical logic of technological systems. As soon as the human being has found his own life path, and is no longer steered by external constraints and fear of punishment, the great shift begins. An essential change of the steering and energy systems occurs; it is the shift from being regulated by outer pressure to the self-regulation of life.

Children learn their native language without having to study vocabulary. They learn by themselves when they are intrinsically motivated to do so. They are perfectly capable of developing their own games, their own rules, their own circus or theater when they are not forced toward perfection. By themselves – by their own volition – adults give their all when they have a compelling objective. Last but not least, our sexual organs always work by themselves when they are liberated from pressure. Sexual impotence vanishes once the body is free of any constraints.

Self-regulation also takes place in the community as soon as sufficient trust is established. Individual decision makers are replaced by the higher intelligence we might call the "communitarian self." The communitarian self works through the individual participants and organizes the community's interests informally and without force. When the members of a community are united by a common plan they can perform miracles of manifestation, as we saw in in the Colombian peace community San José de Apartadó when they built their new center in Mulatos in only a few weeks. They trekked with all the required building materials and machines on long, barely passable tracks through the mountains to the middle of the jungle, far from any streets or power lines, to create their new center for contemplation and study.[3]

I assume that in a few years we will see more and more Healing Biotopes arising by themselves all over the world because a coherent spiritual blueprint for Terra Nova will have spread.

The principle of self-regulation spares us much work. If we succeed in making our actions, thoughts, and movements compatible with the guidance system of the Sacred Matrix we will achieve without effort the aims that would otherwise demand great strength and toil. The by-itself principle is described and perfected within Zen Buddhism and by spiritual masters of the East, the yogis and samurais. They have demonstrated the spectacular achievements man is capable of when he has learned this world principle, described within the Zen tradition as "wu wei" and "mo chi chu." After many years of training, Eugen Herrigel hits the bulls-eye with his arrow because he had learned to remove himself from the process, to get out of the way.[4] This principle, practiced over centuries in the East, seems hardly attainable to us in the West, for we are still trapped in the thinking patterns of the materialistic era. And yet it is the principle of universal life; everything grows, blossoms, works, and multiplies by itself, freely vibrating without stress. Every bee and every spider performs its miracle according to this principle. The spider's web, the eel's journey, the bat's flight, the salmon's jump up the waterfall – everything functions in harmony with this "high-tech" principle of biotechnology. We encounter this modus operandi, which effortlessly achieves maximum precision everywhere in nature. Nature achieves its miracles not through toil or stress, but through sensation, whirl, and oscillation.

I believe that the humanity of the future will be firmly aligned with this principle. We will learn to apply the cosmic functional logic to our upcoming tasks; it is likely to offer interesting insights to even our economic questions: would nature's operating principles not reveal a truly functioning global economic model? The cosmos assembles its structure by itself; no sweating engineer has ever stood beside it. Everything is done through "not-doing." "Wu wei" and "mo chi chu" are not just principles for archery and arranging flowers, but for evolving in the cosmic atelier of a new creation, Terra Nova. In the 1990s we hosted some "desert camps" on La Graciosa, a small island within the Canary Islands, under the Taoist motto: *"When not-doing is accomplished, nothing remains undone."*[5] In the "monasteries" of the future we will study and practice this principle of Zen Buddhism.

The Universal Frequency and the Alpha System

The world is a vibrating system. All things communicate with one another through frequencies. All of life is connected through a universal frequency. We experience this basic vibration when we are in the mode of total trust. We can call it the *Alpha frequency*. It is the frequency of the meta-world. We may also call it the frequency of eternity, or the frequency of God. **It is the vibration of the one existence and one consciousness, which is the same in everything.** That which was once accessed through mystical experience is today the focus of science and tomorrow will give all our social structures direction. The encounter with the "one" was the basis of all authentic religions and philosophies; it is also a cornerstone of our healing theory. Yet we do not need to seek this "one" in religious experiences for it exists also in our everyday life, everywhere hearts open in genuine trust. The "one" is always present even when obscured by a thousand layers. Even when the frequencies of anger, aggression, or fear are in the foreground, the universal frequency is present internally. No organism could live without it. In order to access the healing qualities of the universal frequency we need to take down the walls of separation and clear the psychological minefields, the remains of our history of war that blocks our relationships. We always return to the same fundamental issue: establishing trust.

In the hum of the universal vibration, the power of life and love evolves from moment to moment. When we live in this frequency, trust arises in relation to people and animals. The objective ethics of truth, mutual support, solidarity, and love, become the norm. No human being attuned to the universal frequency could lie to or betray another person, or torment an animal. The universal frequency activates the basic entelechy of all beings. It contains the entire informational matrix of peace and thereby generates genuine peace, for it is in resonance with all that exists. If a project compatible with the universal frequency arises, this project will affect the entire world. If this project contains new information relevant for global evolution, this information will spread all over the Earth. A new field will arise. Now the morphogenetic process will set in and by itself cause this shift, which would through almost any other means remain unattainable. (See Chapter 30).

As a result of its catastrophic history, the human race has drifted beyond the range of the Alpha frequency's influence. Most of our societal systems of politics, economy, religion, and ethics are no longer in resonance with the universal Alpha order. This is why worldwide dissonance persists in the form of individual and pandemic disease, famine, destruction of nature, violence, and war. It is as a result of our distance from the Alpha resonance that we see also the common psychological difficulties of our time, such as heartache, loneliness, depression, epidemic hatred, and mental illness. We have all known these problems and have tried to overcome them through diverse ideological, therapeutic, or religious means. **These attempts will only succeed when we rejoin the universal frequency of life together. In order to do this we need to relieve our souls from the pressure of unresolved pain.** The Alpha frequency will permeate the human organism entirely as soon as the first communities have dissolved this traumatic knot.

The Alpha system is a guidance system, always present, always enabled; it is just that we are for the most part operating in another frequency. *"I am always with you, yet you are so seldom at home"* – one begins to understands what Master Eckhart meant when he let God speak these words through him.[6] Those who live in the Alpha frequency and remain receptive to its information are always protected. Even in the darkest nights, one will find the way without running into obstacles. It seems like a similar principle at work as that which gives orientation to bats. On his search for God, Satprem tested this magic by walking barefoot in the Amazon jungle in the knowledge that it was full of snakes, poisonous spiders, and many other creatures. Nothing harmed him. He had had similar experiences in a concentration camp. He summarized them in a tremendous vision. He says...

There are moments in life when, all of a sudden, you are invincible – absolutely nothing can touch you. If you are on a battlefield, you feel you can go through a hail of bullets unharmed. If you are in the middle of a storm at sea, you laugh and you know that, somehow, you'll make it through those enormous waves. Assassins are sent to kill you, and something in you remains so perfectly still, as if the whole thing were a comedy – they couldn't possibly touch you. And the assassins actually can't touch you.

In one form or another, a lot of people have had this experience: you are suddenly outside the 'law.' You are outside all that seems inevitable – you slip through the meshes. (...) In other words, for a few seconds, those beings who've had this kind of experience have slipped through (...) the web, and so nothing touched them. Nothing can touch them.[7]

I recall also the words that Lao Tsu wrote over 2500 years ago, "*He who knows the truth of existence does not fear wild bulls or tigers...*"[8]

What is described here is not actually an exception, but an elementary fact of life. If we establish new space-time systems for our lives, leading us through their spiritual magnetism into the Alpha frequency, a hologram of protection and healing manifests itself. We stand within a cosmic principle of protection and healing when we rid ourselves of old fears. The protection also applies to psychological health. Whoever stays on the Alpha wave cannot be hurt psychologically. Peace Pilgrim, the modern-day American sage who walked for peace, expressed this so compellingly that I want to quote her here...

No outward thing – nothing, nobody from without – can hurt me inside, psychologically. I recognized that I could only be hurt psychologically by my own wrong actions, which I have control over; by my own wrong reactions – they are tricky but I have control over them, too; or by my own inaction in some situations, like the present world situation, that needs actions from me. (...) You have complete control over whether or not you will be hurt psychologically, and any time you want to, you can stop hurting yourself.[9]

PART III
THE WORLD CAN BE HEALED

Can we imagine living in another form of existence, for example as a Tuareg in Africa, a coca farmer in Colombia, or as an animal – a dolphin, a bird, or a rat? All these forms of existence belong to the great family of life. Each is an organ of the whole. These organs need to be in order and in harmony with each other for the whole to function. Even small creatures, so-called vermin, are organs of the whole and participate in the great work of creation. Whatever we human beings do to other organs in terms of care, help, or violence will return to us as blessings or disease. This points to a first condition for a future without war: we need to step out of the old patterns of isolation and enter the consciousness of unity and compassion. We need to enter into a new "biospheric" consciousness of the cohesiveness of and cooperation between all life on Earth. The basis of this shift is found through insight and awakening love. This is why we need facilities for the development of insight and love on a planetary scale. The building of these facilities is the next step in the transformation that humanity is currently going through. We call these facilities "Healing Biotopes."

Chapter 15: The Earth Needs New Information

Every living organism responds to information. A simple example might illustrate this. I am sitting at my desk working on this book. Someone is using a chainsaw outside. This annoying noise disrupts my calmness. I then find out that the work with the chainsaw is necessary for the development of the Healing Biotope. My organism calms down straight away. A simple piece of information has not only shifted my temper, but my entire being. My organism is a complex system composed of trillions of cells. The entire system responds to a single piece of information!

This process, ostensibly so mundane that we do not stop to reflect on it, becomes immediately significant when we apply the principle to the greater organism of humankind. The entire organism will transform if we insert information that is compatible with the system of the whole. Our focus is on the information of Terra Nova.

Right information saves lives. In 1995 we bought 330 acres of arid land with the intention of turning it into an ecological paradise. Today visitors to Tamera can see the success of our efforts. What is happening here seems miraculous. Healing information existed within the degraded terrain. From a dried out, eroded landscape, a healthy biotope with lush flora and fauna is appearing. More and more birds and animals have returned. Now there are over one hundred species of bird; in the beginning it was far less. Now stinging nettles, a sign of healthy soil, grow all over; in the beginning there were none. It is incredible to watch the emergence of a blooming world from a spoiled landscape. We need courage, intelligence, and wisdom to apply this "miraculous" environmental healing to human beings. **Just as a blossoming ecosystem can emerge from a dying landscape so too can a blossoming human community emerge from a desolate society.** For this to happen the right trigger is needed to activate the intact core of the group members. The principle of healing applies to nature, to human community, and to every individual. **With every disease there exists healing information.** The information that every disease is curable can save lives but it must become known in order for it to be effective. When a patient receives a diagnosis of lung cancer he is overtaken by the fear of death unless he knows that every disease, even every form of cancer, can be healed. It is a necessity to know this and spread this information. All students of the Terra Nova School should know this; every disease can be healed.

The olive tree in my garden has emerged from an invisible substance we call "information." Information lies in the structure of its genetic code located in the seed. I myself have emerged from such a substance. Is it possible that, in principle, everything has evolved from information? If we today move toward a new Earth, is the new information already present somewhere in the invisible world, perhaps in the realm David Bohm called the "implicate order?"[1] Does the image of the new Earth exist somewhere in the universe, just as the "image" of the olive tree is in the genetic material of its seeds? Can we imagine that in a person who is ill, or one with depression or psychosis, there is an intact matrix, hiding like the information of the butterfly within the caterpillar, and that he will heal when we manage to activate this intact matrix? This question was answered by healing experiences we had during the early years of our project in Leuterstal and Schwand (southern Germany). Yes it is possible, on the condition that the patient is embedded in an environment of active healing. Every patient is thus part of a group, and is therefore perfused with collective energies. When those energies correspond to healing powers, healing will come about. The universe takes care of its children so long as the channel is open and we do not block it with wrong information. If our focus is set on the Sacred Matrix then the healing possibilities of the universe will manifest within us. Jesus of Nazareth, Bruno Groening, Adam Dreamhealer, and John of God are examples of the healing miracles, which are always within reach when we are in the sacred healing space.

I would like to summarize this briefly once again: the operative universal powers consist of invisible fields of energy and information. Everything that surrounds us has been generated by these fields. It was particular patterns of information that shaped the old world and brought worldwide violence into being. In a similar way, new informational patterns are bringing about the new world. These patterns are not hypothetical; they are latent in the genetic material of life and in the "cosmic database" of the universe. We have the potential and the freedom to discover them and to bring them to life in new systems. **If this occurs in one location, it becomes a latent occurrence everywhere, for all beings of the Earth are united in a network of living information, a biological and spiritual "internet," a "genetic bio-field."**

During millennia of patriarchy, humanity sent messages of hostility against the body and against womankind into the world. Whoever held power over directing sexual energies held power over all else. Over the course of imperial dominance, information systems came into being which brought humanity into submission. The process operated through the inculcation of concepts such as the sinfulness of the "lust for flesh." With this information, generations were forced into sexual repression, disguise, and lying; witches were burned and old mysteries destroyed. Another concept implied that "jealousy belongs to love." It is through this that Hollywood dramas became icons for millions of love relationships – too often with fatal consequences. Another piece of information that has become deeply rooted in the human psyche is that "war is part of life;" this enabled war to overrun the Earth like an inescapable destiny. With the doctrine that "salvation is not to be found on Earth, but in heaven alone," billions of people could be driven into unspeakable misery. It was religious, moralistic, or political information that forced humanity into submission. And informational fields were what enabled the powers that be to stabilize and expand their dominance. It will take a new field of information to introduce a new era in the evolution of human society.

The old information of fear and violence needs to be replaced with a configuration of trust and cooperation. The capacity for such a fundamental shift is rooted in the structure of creation itself and in our own genetic makeup. As participants in the universe, all of its powers and information are potentially at our disposal. The choices as to what information, which faculties and abilities, we recall depend on our mental and spiritual condition. Our possibilities are boundless, for we live in a boundless universe. Just how far human potential reaches beyond our usual mindset is demonstrated in every quality acrobatic performance. When one after the other joins to build a human pyramid, and yet another climbs on top, we think, "this cannot be possible!" And yet it happens. When free climbers scale overhanging rocks, appearing to ignore the laws of gravity, an unusual power must be at play. The extraordinary performances in the realms of sport, technology, and science reveal the almost unlimited range of human possibilities. That which manifests, the new realities that arise, depend on the information with which we encounter the world. When the following chapters refer to "Water Retention Landscapes" or "*free sexuality*" (see Glossary) or the "immanent God," then key pieces of information capable of transforming the hologram of violence to the hologram of peace are addressed.

The assignment of today's peace workers is to develop ways of living in which the information of peace, solidarity, and cooperation are activated to the point at which these qualities become automatically expressed in our personal and political actions. If we were to succeed in entering such information fields into the biological and spiritual

Internet of humanity we would create a fundamental change in life on our planet. **Thinking along these lines, it is easily conceivable that a planetary society develops whose participants are no longer psychologically or physiologically predisposed to violent actions because they no longer receive impulses that steer them in this direction.** They live in a different hologram. From the many possibilities within the cosmic database, the hologram of healing, solidarity, and love manifests. It may sound like a dream, but it is achievable as a reality. What can be thought can be done.

Flipping the Global Switch

To free the world from violence and war we need to flip a global switch. This is a switch that determines whether holograms of fear and violence or holograms of trust and cooperation are downloaded from the cosmic database. Both possibilities are held in the universe, as they are in the genetic code. We could theoretically "switch off" global war within a short period of time by fully activating the information of peace. If this happens in some groups it happens (latently) everywhere, for as was stated above, all beings are interconnected in the bio-field. **When the informational matrix of peace becomes more powerful than the information of violence, the guiding impulses of violence in the human genetic system will be extinguished. The vile war epoch would thereby come to its end. Through a history of murderous violence, humanity's genetic system switched to a mode of fear and withdrawal; through elementary processes of trust and building community it will shift to cooperation and solidarity. We can give evolution a new direction when we succeed in flipping this central switch and entering new information into our genetic systems.**

The unconscious impulses which drive much of humanity's activity originate in those areas of life that were most traumatized and distorted by the long history of war – the areas of Eros and religion. These are the energetic centers from which a new course must be set. The soul is most sensitive in the realm of sex and love. We need a form of coexistence that allows enough time and calmness for people to see and recognize one another; one that, in the case of an intimate sexual connection, allows leisure to cultivate what is necessary for the soul to settle and expand. After a woman has fully revealed herself sexually to a man she needs a space that enables both partners to integrate the truth they have just experienced. These, often tiny, situations in people's private lives are those that frequently determine whether the information of peace or its opposite arises in the psyche of a community. The more a group develops genuine sensitivity in this area and the more true peace can enter the relationship between the genders, the more powerful their outward effect will be. The switch that needs to be flipped on a global scale is usually located in the intimate realms of our interpersonal relationships.

We can activate the information of peace with every small action. The new concept of global healing can be transformed in each moment into new concepts that guide each of our smallest decisions. The global revolution is connected with quietly revolutionizing our daily lives. Large-scale war is resolved through being recognized and overcome on the small scale. The political and the private are inextricably enmeshed here. The commitment to the humane revolution requires an ethical decision in the interpersonal sphere. The peace worker generates peace in his own house. He can no longer afford to betray another.

The inner decision referred to here should be made very consciously, for today's humane revolution is confronted with reactionary counter powers at every turn – including those from within. The new revolutionaries therefore require great strength and determination to overcome many old habits. The inner switch that we have set toward peace and healing – toward reconciliation instead of revenge, cooperation instead of separation, solidarity instead of competition – can easily flip back. A high degree of continuity and will power is required to deter it from this habit. It will no longer flip back when the objective of the humane revolution has entered the hearts of the activists. Each individual that steps into this space of consciousness gains system-changing power. A community composed of such people and a global network composed of such communities will give rise to a morphogenetic field, flipping the switch all over the globe.

For some time, military laboratories have been working on secret technologies that reach far beyond the scope of conventional technology (e.g. the US military's Philadelphia experiment in 1943, HAARP, et cetera). It is essential that global peace workers do to not react with projections of the occult toward technologies such as these, but instead respond with determination to use this kind of "secret" faculty to activate a global field of peace. These secret powers (powers of attraction, of resonance, of force fields) really do exist; they are inherent to life itself. Psychic powers are at our disposal if we are able recall and utilize them. **We are working to overcome the collective barrier against thinking which has hindered generations from a similar mental and spiritual development in the intrapersonal and interpersonal realms as in the arena of science and technology.** We human beings have caused the suffering on Earth; from a higher perspective it is self-evident that we need to and are able to reverse it.

With the decision to "switch off" war we rank ourselves alongside those people who make radical, life-long commitments to peace. I am thinking of, for example Gloria Cuartas, the former mayor of the Colombian city Apartadó, or Eduar Lanchero, speaker of San José de Apartadó, the renowned peace community with 1700 inhabitants, from which almost two hundred have in recent years been murdered by the military and paramilitary. During a peace pilgrimage that San José and Tamera carried out in Bogotá, Eduar stated,

> *The armed groups are not the only ones who kill. It is the logic behind the whole system. The way people live generates this kind of death. This is why we decided to live in a way that our life generates life. One basic condition, which kept us alive, was to not play the game of fear imposed upon us by the murders of the armed forces. We have made our choice. We chose life. Life corrects and guides us.*[2]

Eduar died from a severe illness in 2012. The burden of the peace mandate he needed to carry in war-stricken Colombia eventually became too heavy. We remain connected to him. He, like Etty Hillesum, is part of our cosmic family.

Chapter 16: Healing in the Spirit of Oneness

A human being is a part of the whole, called by us "Universe," a part limited in time and space. He experiences himself, his thoughts and feelings as something separated from the rest, a kind of optical delusion of his consciousness. This delusion is a kind of prison for us, restricting us to our personal desires and to affection for a few persons nearest to us. Our task must be to free ourselves from this prison by widening our circle of compassion to embrace all living creatures and the whole of nature in its beauty.[1]

~ Albert Einstein

The writer Juergen Dahl narrates the wonderful story of the symbiosis between the bee and the sage plant.[2] It is not a fictional story, but a scientific observation. He describes how the two species are tailored to one another in the minutest detail. Where does this come from? Did a great creator invent the sage first and then develop an insect perfectly adapted to it? Was it the other way around? Or is it simply a coincidence? In this example we recognize what a wonder creation is. It is not only the bee and the sage; all beings cohere with the whole down to the smallest details. Together they form a unity like that between the bee and the sage. Why does nature produce fruits that are "coincidently" delicious to human beings? Because the human being is one with nature. Why are humans equipped with cognitive organs with which we gain insight into the world? Because the human being is one with the world. Goethe brought the idea of unity into the sentence, *"Were the eye not sun-like in itself, how could we see the sun?"*[3] It is a true mystery until one recognizes that it refers to the unity of the world.

In the spiritual domain the forces of healing work through reconnection with the whole. As soon as we are in this realm of oneness we are connected to that "something" that always heals. This something is within all beings. The laws of spiritual healing operate autonomically in this realm. We find ourselves in the space of oneness when we love, when we work creatively, and when we are focused on a higher goal. All of life is associated with this original power field. Only human beings are capable of withdrawing from it. However, we also have the option of reentering this field with another level of consciousness. The "Return of the Prodigal Son"[4] occurs now – in the post-materialistic epoch – as an ethical, social, ecological, and political imperative. By returning to the spiritual realm of oneness, the human being opens to forms of healing inaccessible to him in the conventional biological and medical laws. These ways of healing are of course not new; they have been demonstrated to us by many healers. The shift from the physical to the spiritual dimension of healing is an aspect of the central system change we are going through today. This is what I mean by the term "transformation."

The opening of the sacred space of oneness activates spiritual powers capable of reshaping material structures and of healing even the most serious illnesses. K.O. Schmidt describes the successful spiritual healing of a woman that had suffered from breast cancer. Suddenly a piercing pain traveled through her, after which the knot in her breast was gone. K.O. Schmidt concludes…

> *Is it possible, through spiritual ways of healing, to send a stream of divine love and divine life through soul and body which touches the realm of spiritual energy beyond the atoms and returns the atoms to their original, harmonious order, transforming the molecules in the twinkling of an eye?*

> *Perhaps, when we put our hand into the hand of God and open up to the healing light, we touch the invisible, subatomic realm. In ways still unknown to us we thereby bring these electrons, protons, and neutrons into harmonious relation with one another and without time perceivably passing the cells of the body are immediately returned to their normal condition. Could it not be that way? It would not be beyond my grasp.*

> *Spirit is the origin of human life. Our mental and spiritual imagination folds back to the body. If spirit arises beyond the Earthly, finer, higher frequencies pulses through the building of cells and bring about health. This is undoubtedly the effectiveness of laws, therefore no miracle, but reality, because alongside the laws of physics there are the equally unchangeable laws of spirit, of the spiritual world.[5]*

If we struggle to comprehend the impact of spiritual powers on the material world, we can consider that at the micro scale material is not made of matter. At the subatomic level, precisely there where we have searched for the essence of matter, modern physics refers to energy fields or *fields of potentiality* **(see Glossary). The material world is not composed of tiny particles, but fields. Thus it becomes quite imaginable that such fields are changed by the permeation of spiritual powers.** I believe this understanding to be a basic element of the upcoming worldview. Spiritual healing will thus not be the exception, but the norm. We will heal by creating fields of sacred spirit. Every future community will be carried by this spirit. What today still seems unrealistic and divorced from reality will soon be common knowledge, for it is the way of collective healing.

Collective Healing

One area of spiritual healing work is distance healing. The spiritual long-distance effect takes place when the spiritual transmission (a thought or image) meets a corresponding point of reception in the consciousness of a person. Distance healing can also be applied to groups or whole regions. In order to be effective, healing information sent into the world must address the "collective subconscious." The overarching information of Healing Biotopes, which we want to send into the world, will become effective when it is received in the collective subconscious of humanity, activating the archetypal picture of an intact world. This works – as has been described above – when the information sent is compatible with the Sacred Matrix, which all human beings carry as a genetic pattern within themselves.

The phenomenon of mass healing is a special form of collective healing. The happenings at the mass gatherings of the American preacher Kathryn Kuhlman or the German miracle healer Bruno Groening show the power with which a healing message can enter people when a collective field is generated. Many people seen as incurably ill were suddenly healed. People walking with crutches put their crutches aside, paraplegics left their beds, those dependent on wheelchairs got up and walked, and the blind saw. I think this can teach us a great deal for the upcoming healing and peace work. The impossible becomes possible when we open other mental and spiritual doors.

We are facing a new assignment to spread knowledge in the current digital age. Awoken by the miracle of the digital world, we approach those similar miracles that require no technologies – the miracles of the spiritual world: the phenomena of spiritual information transmission, of telepathy and telekinesis, spiritual healing and distance healing, the wonders of prayers finding fulfillment, of spiritual guidance, and of new connections in the circuit of the universe. Evolution will not stop with the digital age. This could be the prelude to an era in which digital information technology is, bit by bit, complimented or even superseded by spiritual information systems.

Why do Religious, Therapeutic, and Moral Appeals Fail?

We are about to set out into a new world of spiritual healing for those near and far – for human beings, animals, landscapes, waters, and eventually the entire planet – but this triumphal march of spirit demands a different societal foundation. K.O. Schmidt, representatives of "New Thought," and many others have time and again tried to initiate a worldwide healing movement. It has not come to be, for societal conditions have not allowed it. The concept of spiritual healing remains accessible to only a few people. A society in which people mistrust one another does not support spiritual healing. In the framework of the existing relations of production and power, spiritual healing exclusively remains a peripheral issue for some specialists.

Humanity has long sought healing and redemption. To this end we have developed many religious and therapeutic systems; we have tried following the "Sermon of the Mount," the guidance of Buddhism, of bioenergetics, of positive thinking and so on. None of these systems have had long-lasting success, for the simple reason that they addressed the individual, not society. The societal causes of misery were not removed. The sick or evil individual was healed, but not the society that had generated sickness and evil. This was a fundamental flaw that foiled even our best efforts, for hardly anyone could be permanently faithful to the ethical and spiritual precepts of the divine within a society founded on war. To enable sustainable, long-term healing and liberation, the structures of society must be changed. Healing and redemption is thereby revealed as a social, political, and revolutionary issue.

This is the parting of the ways. Many people have wanted to lead a new and good life, but few were ready to step out of the old societal tracks. We have thereby remained in the old dichotomy – with on one side the "good," leading ethical private lives, and on the other, the revolutionaries who abandon morality so as to reach their political goals. A new kind of revolutionary is now needed; one who changes society while following ethical guidelines because he has experienced life and love.

Chapter 17: It is Life Itself that Heals

The French resistance fighter Jacques Lusseyran wrote a formidable report of the healing he experienced in the Buchenwald concentration camp. He was fatally ill and was left in the mortuary. There he observed, with full consciousness, as one organ after the next failed until he should have surely been dead. He was not dead however, but fully experienced life for the first time. He writes…

I watched the stages of my own illness quite clearly. I saw the organs of my body blocked up losing control one after the other, first my lungs, then my intestines, then my ears, all my muscles, and last of all my heart, which was functioning badly and filled me with a vast, unusual sound. I knew exactly what it was, this thing I was watching: my body in the act of leaving this world, not wanting to leave it right away, not even wanting to leave it at all. I could tell by the pain my body was causing me, twisting and turning in every direction like snakes that have been cut through.

Have I said that death was already there? If I have I was wrong. Sickness and pain, yes, but not death. Quite the opposite, life, and that was the unbelievable thing that had taken possession of me. I had never lived so fully before. Life had become a substance within me. It broke into my cage, pushed by a force a thousand times stronger than I... I drew my strength from the spring. I kept on drinking and drinking still more... That was the one battle I had to fight, hard and wonderful all at once: not to let my body be taken by the fear. For fear kills, and joy maintains life.[1]

Lusseyran recovered soon after. It was not medicine that healed him; it was life itself! Life is unfathomable, unlimited, and eternal. It is the unknown variable beyond all things. It shines with a sacred light originating from unknown sources. Life itself is full of healing powers, which are not yet explained by science. It is life that carries out miraculous healing in the same way as it carries out all the other daily miracles: sprouting plants, bleating sheep, playing children. Life itself is the unknown master who generates and directs this all. All the magnificence we have projected into God belongs to life itself.

Love is a particularly intimate state of being in life in which very special healing powers become effective. Arcady Petrov represents a group of doctors in Moscow who are carrying out pioneering work in this field. Petrov describes the case of a man so severely injured in a car accident that he had no medical chance of survival. With the help of a nurse with psychic ability, the medics activated the man's love for his two-year-old daughter. His organs suddenly began working again; the patient became healthy and was released from the hospital after only four weeks.[2] It was love that guided his entire organism from imminent death back to life! Life and love are healing powers par excellence as soon as they are freed from all cages and blockages. We hold the achievement of lasting love as a primary goal in our work. Do we have enough power within us to imagine a world driven by the essential forces of life and love?

The Principle of Self-Healing

We can picture the universe as a giant organism, which constantly receives information from its organs and returns corresponding impulses. Whenever a disturbance occurs anywhere, powers are mobilized, like in a cybernetic circuit, to remove it. When people create wounds in nature, through for example mines and quarries, the healing forces of the Sacred Matrix are set into motion. **At the point of injury healing plants arise; the biotope cures itself.** The information necessary for healing the place is recalled from the cosmos and activated. This is the self-healing and self-organization we can observe everywhere in nature, including our own bodies. When I have cut my finger cellular processes instantly begin operating to close the wound. The organism knows which correction is needed. We ourselves are this organism; we actually know what corrections are necessary and how our human life would look if it were in order. The idea of planetary Healing Biotopes developed from the application of these observations to the social and political realm.

Where nature is destroyed to the degree that it can no longer receive and make manifest the cosmic information of the Sacred Matrix, we can help it along by giving a "kick," restoring its receptiveness to healing information and to its inherent impulses. We can do this by, for example, creating a Water Retention Landscape on degraded land, as seen in the work of the aforementioned Austrian ecologist Sepp Holzer.[3] Nature responds immediately, and in a short time we might have, depending on our intention, a blossoming landscape or a fertile Permaculture farm.

The human organism is, in like manner, no longer able to fully absorb cosmic healing information because our channels are blocked. We are blocked by what Wilhelm Reich refers to as *body armor* (see Glossary) in the heart, belly, and sexual areas, but above all, by the collective trauma which is written into our entire cellular system. In order to restore the receptiveness of the human organism to cosmic healing, it needs a kick strong enough to dissolve the old blockages. This kick could be an experience of love, of death, of God, or of witnessing misery in crisis areas. It could be a decision to work, an observation of animals, an experience of a functioning community, or of friendship. Participation in a collective peace action or in the creation of Terra Nova can also restore our connection to cosmic healing information.

It is often serious strokes of fate that provide this kick, reshaping life from its foundation. In addition to our personal misfortunes, global strokes of fate affect us all. If we are awake enough, they can rid us of our blockages and guide us to a new task in life. Alongside all existential tremors, there is an obvious truth: self-healing powers are always activated when a feeling of well-being arises in the patient. It can be that a single word of acknowledgement that a sick person receives from their beloved sets their soul's self-healing powers so strongly into motion that all illness vanishes. **Healing occurs in the moment we enter information into an ailing organism that is able to activate its self-healing powers.**

These thoughts are at the core of individual and global healing work. They are basic thoughts of the project for a new Earth as they convey an image for the upcoming revolution. The revolution ahead of us will no longer play out primarily on the political stage, but on an energetic, ethical, and noetic one. It will no longer consist primarily of a change in political power, but in creating new social systems for the activation of the immanent healing powers of all its participants. It will no longer work through violence, but by creating new communication systems on the basis of trust. Once they are globally linked, they will overcome the existing economic and political power systems.

Chapter 18: Healing by Activating the Original Matrix

Every being is integrated within the universal order of the Sacred Matrix according to its own original matrix. When we stimulate a sick organism in such a way that it comes into resonance with the frequency of the Sacred Matrix, all its cells arrange themselves in a healing manner in accordance with its entelechy, i.e. its original matrix. In the order of the world there is also an original matrix for human community. This is depicted symbolically in the stone circle of Almendres, near Évora in Portugal. We have often visited this monument to study under the guidance of Sabine Lichtenfels. We encountered a primordial social system that even today carries a message for the future. We call it the *prehistoric utopia* (see Chapter 24). Sabine Lichtenfels has described the *prehistoric utopia* in detail in her book *Traumsteine* [Dream Stones]. In a meditation at the stone circle she received the following information:

> *It is important for you to rediscover the information that is laid out in the code of creation and is necessary for creating a more complete world. Over thousands of years it has been forgotten and distorted. This has had horrible consequences for life on Earth and for the Earth itself. You will find gathered here all the necessary information for building a tribe. It is similarly effective in creating a genetic code for a nonviolent culture.* [1]

When we establish a Healing Biotope we activate the original matrix of community in accordance with the universal concept of human coexistence and of coexistence with the beings of nature. When a new planetary community develops, one that follows the principles of the great order of life, a tremendous field of power for a new connection between human society and the healing powers of the universe arises on Earth.

The Entelechy Program

The soul of the world carries a dream, which is imprinted in all beings as an image of its entelechy. The short poem of Josef von Eichendorff attests to this:

Sleeps a song in things abounding
That keeps dreaming to be heard:
Earth's tunes will start resounding
If you find the magic word.[2]

The Sacred Matrix is anchored in the nuclei of our cells as the basic entelechy pattern of our life. Every living being follows its entelechy program. In it lies the genetic template for its development and goal. This "entelechy drive" has great strength. The entelechy is what makes the fragile seedling capable of breaking through the thick layer of asphalt. Whatever resistance it faces, it will continue growing with all its strength. The entelechy program always prevails. Those in power needed to work hard to break their subjects' entelechy drive. What remains is an insatiable yearning for a life that is not possible under these conditions: a longing for sex, love, and home. The longing will endure until the human being recognizes his dream and brings it to fruition.

We are, within certain bounds, free to stray from the path to our entelechy, but if we wander too far we perish. Today humanity is at a dangerous edge. It has lost sight of its entelechy and needs to find it again. Every individual is challenged to find his own entelechy again and to follow his "inner voice" more than the inclinations of his social milieu. The entelechy program of the individual leads him to his assigned position within the cosmic plan, or as the leprosy doctor Ruth Pfau said, *"the place where God wants me to be."*[3] We are all, no matter what detours we take, on the way to the right place. It is an ethical, social, and spiritual path that I refer to here. When we are on this path, living in accordance with our entelechy, we become aware of the joy and "rightness" of our actions. The program is always activated when people adopt a disposition of helping or love to one another or toward the beings of nature. All beings react positively to assistance and friendliness, even if they do not show it. Following the entelechy program is often not conscious; one does it instinctively. Our mind, spirit, and body mostly "know" what needs to be done.

To live according to our entelechy is to live under the guidance of our own "knowing." It is as if we are connected with a cosmic "all-knowingness" like a car is connected to the omniscience of the GPS navigator. The GPS knows the destination and the way to reach it; it also recognizes the detours and what needs to be done when one has made a mistake. It is an astonishing analogy for the experience of divine guidance. Jacques Lusseyran described very precisely how this works in daily life. He was blind, unable to see with his physical eyes, but always saw what had to be done on something like an inner screen. When he was on the right track light appeared; when he was off track, it darkened. This applied both to his physiological and psychological orientation. He could always orient toward the light and find the way; in other words, he was always under guidance. Lusseyran's experience coheres with what I refer to in this book as the Alpha frequency. When he was angry, malevolent, or fearful, his screen became dark and he lost orientation; he bumped into a table, stumbled, and walked into the tree. It is worthwhile reading his book, *And There Was Light*, for it provides answers to a number of questions about life and healing.[4] It is one of the very rare books that give such a direct impression of what is possible when one remains open to what the universe offers.

Given that all beings are connected in the universal frequency, all are therefore in communication with one another. The entelechy of life **guides all beings toward contact and communication, trust and love, not toward fear and separation.** However, in today's societies, the latter is more often the case, for life in these aberrant, globalized systems is incompatible with the path laid out by our entelechy. The human being of our time does not move like a free being, but rather like an amoeba hit with a drop of acetone. As this drop came down again and again, generation after generation, it needed to retract its tentacles, and could therefore no longer follow its entelechy program, which originally geared it toward encounter and contact.

If one day the entire human community manages to connect with its entelechy, which we have also referred to as its collective original matrix, or the *prehistoric utopia* (see Glossary), then the entire human race will undeniably be on the way to healing, for then it will automatically be one with the sacred whole. From this conviction, a daring thought arose at the time of our project's founding: **Would it not be possible to introduce – through an entry in the spiritual internet – a planetary process to liberate all of humanity from its old programs of war and to connect it with the vision of its entelechy?**

Chapter 19: The Healing of Love

In its true sense, learning to live in the right way means learning love. True love does not make claims of possession or any conditions. To my knowledge, the only thing that really heals people is unconditional love. Love is what gives life its meaning.[1]

~ Elisabeth Kübler-Ross

In the heart of humanity's soul lies the immense power of erotic love. Healing love has been at the core of the project's research for nearly forty years, for it is indispensable to global peace work. This is relevant for all forms of love relationships, however throughout my research in this area, I have focused on the love between the genders. In this sense, I ask all of my LGBTQ friends for their understanding as I emphasize the love between man and woman in this chapter.

We invest so much focus on the love between the genders because the man-woman relationship contains particular archetypal energies of polarity. These are fundamental powers of creation. We knew that global suffering can only come to an end when we install a different system of living on Earth from the base up. What is the "base" of human culture? The masculine and the feminine are the two halves of humanity. Their relation is the basis of human culture. It is not just that the masculine and the feminine form the two halves of humanity, but also two poles within the human being. I refer here to the absolute, organic cohesiveness of the genders. This can be experienced in love when suddenly – in the moment of greatest polarity – one recognizes oneself in the other. Tat tvam asi.

The happiness or misery of humanity depends on its two halves meeting in the right way. For so long as this does not happen, we will continue to see social catastrophes. The animal kingdom also suffers from the pain of humanity – the daily massacre of animals in slaughterhouses or laboratories can only occur so long as human beings keep their hearts closed. For thousands of years man and woman searched for and always missed each other. The world lives in heartache. Healing the collective pain in love is an essential challenge of our times. **When the latent war between the genders comes to its end, there will be no more war on Earth.**

There is a wonderful Inuit tale relayed by Clarissa Pinkola Estés in her book *Women Who Run with the Wolves,* which illustrates this well. The story, entitled "The Skeleton Woman," describes the situation that arises when a man sees the heart of a woman after thousands of years of ossifying neglect. The man is a fisherman; the woman is reduced to a bare skeleton. She represents the original nature of woman, which became emaciated, for man gave no resonance to her primal power. As the fisherman sleeps, a tear runs from the corner of his eye. The woman swallows his tear like someone dying of thirst. She knows that, with wordless comprehension, the fisherman has recognized woman's original nature, that his is a tear of boundless empathy and unspeakable regret, the tear of insight. Estés explains, *"Now something else will develop and be reborn within him, something he can give her: a vast and oceanic heart."*[2] Now the woman's soul receives the nourishment she has long yearned for. Now the wondrous healing begins, the transformation of the skeleton into a blossoming woman. Here lies the key. Here lies the point that determines whether there will be war or peace on Earth. Herein lies the opportunity for the world of man to transcend the fossilizing structures of ideology, didacticism, and legislation. Herein lies the opportunity for the masculine to find a new direction, opening to the feminine source, opening for the original nature, for healing and peace for all creatures. The man resulting from this evolutionary decision is not a "softy," but one capable of love, one who is no longer tied to his mother's apron strings.

The unfathomable violence that is perpetrated against humans and animals all over the world is enacted by closed hearts. It is also the will of the banks, secret societies, and multinationals, but their plans can only be implemented by a society that suffers collectively from a closed heart. So long as the two poles of humanity do not meet in the right way, there will be a calamity in our souls that cannot be soothed by wealth and comfort. It is this calamity of unrequited love that, despite all moral or religious appeals, repeatedly produces depravity. Incredible things take place behind the scenes in the bourgeois world. Domestic abuse, marital rape, murder from jealousy, and child abuse are rampant. In what state is the soul of an adult who resorts to intercourse with children in order to satisfy their sexual urges? **Moral outrage does not help here; help is only to be found in the development of a new sexual culture that restores the joy which humankind lost in a world hostile to love.**

There is such bliss when two lovers embrace for the first time. Yet what of it remains after ten years? A fulfilled sexual life, like a fulfilled religious life, is a cornerstone of human happiness. In the first embrace a love becomes visible, a deep joy that sparkles in our depths until it is realized. The two turn into an inseparable "couple" and want to remain so forever. Nothing is more sacred to them than the vow of eternal faithfulness that they make to each other and only to each other. And therein begins the trouble. They do not yet know how to endure the happiness they experience. That which they admire through the projection of sacredness on to each other, this image of the beloved at their very best, requires a great deal of inner work to become the substance of a reliable partnership. They need a very rare kind of knowledge for this. While we have physics, the science of the material world, we do not have the science of love. The society to come needs a **Love School** where people learn how they can transform their initial bliss into a permanent loving power and into sustainable partnership. A love couple that does not have this knowledge will, sooner or later, fail; love too easily degenerates into fear of loss, mistrust, jealousy, and hatred. This is the tragedy behind today's society; it is the same pain passed endlessly from generation to generation.

The core of the healing work of Terra Nova is the creation of a new relationship based on trust and solidarity. In order to be able to reveal themselves to one another, lovers need profound trust, which could barely surface during the patriarchal era. We can liberate the world from war if we are able to end the war in love. We can liberate the Earth from violence if we are able to end violence in sexuality – without suppressing our own wild nature! The passion can stay. Combined with trust, passion does not lead to violence but to spirited tenderness. It is beautifully set out in the scheme of life. Sensual love is the most reliable foundation against violence. Could a boy that has just loved a girl torture a rabbit?

There is something in life that we all love infinitely. If humanity succeeds in giving continuity to this "something," we will have accessed an historic path of happiness. The wisdom of the East has created a beautiful aphorism, *"The Tao is the way that cannot be abandoned. The way that can be abandoned is not the Tao."*[3] What if we replaced the word "Tao" with this ever most deep, knowing love? And this is also always meant physically; knowing love goes through the body and through the flesh because *"the word became flesh, and dwelt among us."*[4] It is downright fantastic how many truths we find in the old books of wisdom, if we look beyond the distortions. The climax is found in the story of The Fall when Adam ate the apple from the tree of knowledge and then discovered sexual pleasure, *"and Adam knew his wife."*[5] In Hebrew they have the same word for knowledge and intercourse. They knew it!

The healing of love seldom happens through face-to-face conversations between partners because they are far too involved in their problem. To become capable of love we must learn not to become wrapped up in ourselves, but to participate in the world or the community we live in. **Participation is a secret of love.** This brings us into the field of ethics. Participation connotes care, assistance, friendliness, and releasing the bolts with which we have locked our hearts. To become capable of love, we must develop a system of life in which real trust between people can arise and flourish. This is the crucial point time and again. The new centers are "greenhouses of trust."

In order to free our community from sexual falsehoods, we in Tamera have explored the concept of "free sexuality" (see Chapter 20). **Yet free love and free sexuality can only be humane among people that trust one another.** It is trust that opens the heart and the body, dissolves the body armor, and heals the soul. We work on environmental and technological issues, healing water, Permaculture, and green energy, but the most important work is the creation of trust among people.

Partnership as an Ideal

Free sexuality does not contradict partnership. Partnership is an ideal expression of love, the path to which is not barred by the principles or practice of free sexuality. The ideological condemnation of marriage is as absurd as the ideological condemnation of free sexuality. Marriage remains a sacrament in the new society but will be based on completely different prerequisites than in former times. Free sexuality offered an antithesis to bourgeois marriage; now we need a synthesis of the two. This is not a question of personal preference but of gaining deeper insight into the essence of erotic love, which leads us to a new understanding, a new image in which free sexuality and partnership are deeply connected. When two people come together on the path of truth and trust, when they no longer react from expectation of loss with the anticipation of separation when the other has a sexual adventure, they can make a bond for life. All those who feel the ardent longing for partnership in their hearts can help to bring this new image to fulfillment. They are working on behalf of the countless others that also know this longing.

SD Forum

We need highly determined communities in order to live lives free from ideology and pretense. The issues connected with sex, love, and partnership are far too complex to be carried by small groups, let alone by just two people. These are historic concerns of humankind. We need communities that understand the matter and agree on a fundamental, absolute solidarity with all those who reveal themselves as they share their experiences. To this end we have introduced a method called *SD Forum* (see Glossary) in our group work. SD stands for "Selbstdarstellung," which is German for self-expression. It is a process in which a performer can show himself, his fears and conflicts, to the group without reservation, free from the threat of condemnation.

The SD Forum is guided by a basic thought, mentioned above, that has yet to be adequately understood. The personal problems we reveal before the group are not private issues, but issues of humanity. Whoever gets stuck in the conflict of his longings and does not know how to go on can understand his issue to be a collective issue and not add it to his private "guilt account." The point is not to suffer from personal turmoil but to recognize the global aspect of it. Those who work conscientiously on their jealousy issues work for all humanity. The idea is for performers to bear witness to the inner workings of issues that currently make our civilization perish and to take corresponding action in support of the global effort. "Insight instead of therapy" was our provocative motto at the beginning of the project.

This is about learning solidarity on a deeper level. When people recognize each other in their shared afflictions, they feel less need to disguise themselves and can live together with greater trust. To be seen is to be loved. This is a true statement but it takes courage to let oneself be seen. We had to develop many unusual methods to find the way of truth in love. We are far from finished, but we may have crossed the halfway point on the bridge. It has been long and sometimes tedious work.

Basic Guidelines

From our research ten basic guidelines for the renewed coexistence of the genders have emerged. They could be included in the ethical foundations of a new culture:

1. Love is the ultimate treasure of human culture.

2. Trust between man and woman is the basis of a future without war. Never lie to your love partner.

3. You can only be faithful if you are allowed to love others. Free love and the love between a couple are not mutually exclusive, but complementary.

4. Jealousy is not part of love.

5. Partnership does not derive from mutual possession, but only from mutual compassion and support.

6. Sadism and masochism are the result of humanity's mistreatment of sexuality. Violence is not part of sexuality and submission does not belong to love.

7. No sex with children.

8. Sexual acts must never be conducted against the will of any person.

9. There is no ownership in love. Relationship problems cannot be solved legally, but only with the help of a supportive community.

10. If you have a choice between love and something else, follow love.

In the behavior of women in Tamera towards men, patterns have emerged, which we might call "gentle feminism." Women begin to explore their feminine source and thus generate their own authority, which no longer depends on the relationship with only one man. This establishes an historic new anchor point for women in the *Holon* (see Glossary) of life and society. In her book *Weiche Macht* [Gentle Power], Sabine Lichtenfels, who heads Tamera's Love School, encapsulates this repositioning in the following way:

> *Over 3,000 years of history bear the imprint of male dominance, establishing a principle of hard power. The power within male-dominated societies lay in breaking resistances, which was expressed through conquests, religious warfare, as well as in their methods of education and in the technological treatment of nature. By using these methods modern man has maneuvered himself into an inner dead-end from which he can no longer escape without female support. We do not intend to reestablish ancient matriarchal structures, nor do we want to dominate or patronize men. Feminine power is not targeted at men, nor is it targeted against our love for men*

*– it simply, decisively leaves behind those male structures
that have led to the worldwide extinction of life and love.
(...) Unless we women take a public stand, nobody can
escape this dead-end. It is up to us women to again
assume the political and sexual responsibility that has
been missing for so long. We invite all dedicated men to
join our peace work.*[6]

Reconnecting with the Christ Nature

The healing of love is not limited to erotic love. It also includes a
new relationship to the fellow human being, to nature, and to all
creatures. We need the reintegration of our human world in the overall
world of life to heal the primal pain of separation. Ultimately this
entails reconnecting with *Omega*, the divine center in all things. To
love is to approach each other "center to center," wrote the Jesuit priest
Pierre Teilhard de Chardin in his great cosmological vision of the
human being.[7] Working on the issue of love leads us to realms of great
intimacy. The further we advance, the more clearly we see in our
partner the qualities of a being that belongs in its entirety to the intact
sacred world. This provokes an interesting shift in our relationship. We
see the "Christ nature" shine through in the other. I have observed that
this being shines through everywhere that fear vanishes and trust arises.
The communities of the future could consist of people that have seen
this figure in each other. **When the Christ nature within the man and
the Marian nature of the woman have recognized one another as
the same, there can no longer be hostility between them.**
This is the true place in which to anchor; here lies the Holy Grail.
The Christ nature in the human being, the Marian nature in the human
being – this is the love story of humanity as it was meant to be, the true
eternal love. We encounter it in erotic love, in love for our friends, in
love for nature, and love for God. In order to find and manifest it on
Earth we defuse our inner mines, abandon once and for all the neurotic
patterns, and open the land for receiving new powers.

Love School

The Love School is part of Tamera's education both internally for
the co-workers of the project, as well as for students from around the
world. The basic thoughts for healing love, sex, and partnership are
explored in courses and intensive seminars. During this time the
participants have the opportunity to reflect on their situation anew,

correct their prejudices, and bring their relationships back into order. What happens here, in a circle of between fifty and one hundred people, in terms of psychological destinies and renewal cannot be captured in words. People in high societal positions reveal their helplessness, their fears, their "abnormal" wishes. For many it is the first time in their lives that they experience being able to speak their most intimate issues to a group. The arena of so-called "perversions" seems to be limitless. In the space of revelations such as these, an agreement not to condemn emerges and within this there are astonishing healing powers. Time and again we experience how quickly and easily people can break free from their old sexual habits once they have better alternatives. For new ways to be sustainable the conditions in which people live need to be changed. The possibility of reaching lasting liberation within the existing systems of work, consumption, and marriage are of course very narrow. We cannot yet offer an answer to this. The solution lies in the participants recognizing the situation and actively joining the movement for a free Earth. They can all actively collaborate in the creation of a humane world by, for example, joining the international Terra Nova School founded by Tamera to establish stations for the Terra Nova movement in all countries.

The Global Love School, an annual gathering led by Sabine Lichtenfels, is an important element of Tamera's Love School. People from different countries come here to work together on the issues of sex, love, and partnership. They experience the conflicts, the inner problems and questions relating to sexual love, as the same all over the world. The morphogenetic field of war burdens the human race; the collective trauma, and erroneous thought patterns have generated the same structures of manifest or latent fear of loss, jealousy, anger, and disappointment everywhere. We see everywhere how initially loving relationships transform, in a world hostile to love, into fields of problem and distress. It is not individuals' mistakes, but a system error that makes it so difficult to find fulfillment in love. This insight leads to a healing de-privatization of so-called personal problems. It is logical that we need to develop another system of living to heal the relationship between the genders. What has so far been seen as a private matter is in reality a public concern and global political issue. Working on our relationships is a great service to society. Human society will only be free once it has solved its love issue. A new culture develops from a new relation between the genders.

The Dō of Love

"Dō" is a sacred path leading to the divine world. People have developed many holy paths throughout history, but rarely have they walked the Dō of erotic love. Humankind can only attain happiness when it finds the Dō of erotic love. Herein lies the real revolutionary focus of our time. In erotic love, the fleshly encounters the sacred; the personal encounters the transpersonal, in the most direct way. The new peace workers will walk the Dō of love. The Dō of love is the Dō of the next era of humanity in which all people will discover one another anew. If through our work we succeed in building a morphogenetic field of the Dō of love, we will offer humanity and eventually the entire Earth the greatest service possible.

What has actually hindered us from recognizing and affirming this truth over so many generations? The creation of Terra Nova corresponds to the awakening from an incredible epoch of hypnosis. People have proclaimed messages of salvation and beaten one another to death; they have worn iron chastity belts at night; they have fasted and suffered to calm their inner drives. But there was a force they could not subdue: the "superpower" of sexuality and the longing for love. Until the day arrived when they awakened from hypnosis, from a satanic delusion under which, against their own wills, men and women for centuries labored in vain. Humanity could not become happy so long as it was forced to reject that which is most beautiful. So long as sensual love was obscured, humanity was destined to search without finding.

When sensual love is brought so strongly into focus, the agonizing question of aging comes up. What should we do when we get older? What sweetness will come to us when the skin has become withered and the face wrinkled? My answer is born out of experience. There is still sexual love in old age. It is the most direct and honest expression of **soul love.** Soul love was given to us at birth as part of our entelechy program. It belongs to our basic psychological nature and is meant to be present at all ages. Soul love led us to the first experience of being in love in our youth or childhood. Later, when this love led to the sexual meeting of two bodies, a kind of happiness beyond words arose. This experience was relegated to the realm of fairytales and naïve, youthful dreams by the frustration within society. Only very few relationships could withstand this and remain faithful to love. Behind all aberrations and confusions a path between man and woman is paved, guiding us to the entelechial place in our lives – the discovery of love.

The soul love between the genders is at the center of human longing. It is women who instinctively follow their birthright of giving physical expression to this love. It will be women that care for the Love Schools in the Healing Biotopes. They will help to restore the wisdom of temple priestesses from former times to modern life. They are working on developing the Dō of love. They will be supported by men to joyfully walk this path. Men too will occasionally offer themselves in the service of love. In this way, on a higher level of order, solidarity arises between the genders and a shared appreciation for those parts of Eros formerly banished to the brothels. So long as this desire for love remains unfulfilled, human beings will continue to build bombs. One who experiences love through body and soul cannot build bombs. *"Make love not war."* This is the answer. Amen.

Chapter 20: Liberating Sexuality

If one asks me where to obtain the deepest insight of that inner essence of the world, which I have called the will for life, or where one obtains the purest revelation of oneself, I need to refer to the lustful delight in the act of copulation. This is it! This is the true essence and core of all things, goal and purpose of all existence.[1]

~ Arthur Schopenhauer

We are astonished by the quote above. It reaches the innermost core so directly in a way that is uncommon in philosophy. At least as astonishing are these words from Teilhard de Chardin: *"The most alive thing you can grasp is flesh. And flesh, for man, is woman."*[2]

Teilhard de Chardin was a priest and paleontologist. He knew the sacred in Eros and he knew the innermost meaning of fleshly lust, even though, as a priest he renounced it. I ask you to reflect on this word for just a moment: "flesh," or to think about the state of being we call "horny." Do you notice an ungraspable arousal, something true, which is too shameful to be spoken out? There where our words suggest the most base, the most elevated and beautiful could be waiting. We do not find it because our culture threw it into the gutter and has so far neglected to retrieve it. The revolution that has just begun must turn the value scale of the old world upside down, to reposition many a thing from the gutter to the very top. The secret of matter is also the secret of flesh and the secret of flesh is a secret of love; the secret of love is the secret of God. The divine world is made manifest in freely lived Eros. And this is what the man encounters with particular radiance in the woman – and vice versa. It is also in the image of the prince that an aspect of the divine world becomes manifested. The archetype of the prince is an erotic light figure for both genders attracting both hetero- and homosexual love.

The basic fact of the genders, the longing of the body, and a great historical trauma all sit at the base of human life. In order to find out how genuine unification arises, many different paths can be taken: the path of polygamy and monogamy, of hetero- and homosexuality, of partnership, free sexuality, and ways connecting both, certainly also paths of celibacy and periods of sexual abstinence, as they were for example walked by Teilhard de Chardin and Pia

Gyger. **No law can dictate the right sexual decision to us; there is only the authentic human experience and the freedom to follow it.** Wherever and however this happens authentically, it is a contribution in the great plan of life. To find our way we need to open to all paths and **eliminate all factors that force us to lie.**

Beyond all opinions lies the magic of sexual desire. To quote a wonderful statement the American author Douglas C. Abrams puts in the mouth of the womanizer Don Juan,

> *I will tell you the reason for my success, and it is not the reasons that have been given – not wealth, nor title, nor beauty. The only secret I have used to unlock the bedchambers of the women I have known is their own unquenched thirst for life. The greatest power in the world, greater than kings and popes, is the desire of women. Love, the priests tell us, rules the heavens, but does desire not rule the Earth? One who understands the workings of desire understands the very secret of life.*[3]

The work of a humane peace movement includes freeing this desire from the narrow cages of bourgeois or religious propriety, and offering it a direction in which it can find fulfillment in freedom and mutual responsibility. The more we recognize how strongly human life is, consciously or unconsciously, steered by this desire the more the issue of sexuality becomes the focus of our thoughts. This is where the deepest system change from the hologram of violence to the hologram of love occurs. Hardly any realm of human existence has been so suppressed, defiled, tormented, distorted, denied, and vilified as sexuality. Almost everywhere, this was done in the name of power, and executed through war, sadism, and unbounded sexual crime. In most cases the victims were women. To this day, the history of sexuality is a history of woman's plight, of feminine suppression, exploitation, and violation. As a result most women no longer want to or can fully affirm their own sexual nature. Sexual revelation and self-revelation is however a condition of **knowing** love. For its enablement, we need men that do not abuse the sexual revelation of the woman, but welcome it in the spirit of partnership and who are willing to answer it with their own revelation. When a woman reveals herself sexually, she gives the most profound offering a woman can give to a man. Men need to learn to deal properly with this. They need to understand the significance of the revelation. When he understands this he will be grateful and feel deep solidarity toward her, even if there is no intention of relationship from either side. There are still only a few such men, for there has not yet been a culture that could raise them.

To create equal sexual emancipation for both men and women, we need functioning communities of trust in which old taboos and prejudices can be overcome at depth.

It is really hard to maintain the old system of marriage and couple-love within community because there are so many potential sexual partners. The sexual desire of most women, like men, reaches far beyond their relationship with a single partner. They need the chance to reveal this desire to each other without fear or shame. Free sexuality is the sexual revelation of both men and women. One of our key phrases was and is, "You can only be faithful if you are also allowed to love others."

The system of free sexuality develops organically from an intact community life. Free sexuality is neither an ideology nor a preconceived program, but a development which emerges on its own, leading toward truth and freedom if we are courageous enough to allow it. No couple living in Tamera for a longer stretch of time has been able to maintain strict monogamy. One slowly discovers that faithfulness stems from a soul connection and cannot be attained by the sexual exclusion of others.

One eventually discovers that free sexuality and partnership do not contradict, but mutually complement one another. This discovery changes lives. If this becomes prevalent it will morphogenetically relieve human civilization from immeasurable pain. Free sexuality and couple love are not mutually exclusive! One need not be jealous when one's partner has an "adventure," for one is allowed to do it oneself. One can experience that this actually does no harm to partnership and love, given it is genuine. The mess takes place only in the head, not in the nature of reality. Jealousy does not belong to love! If a couple manages to maintain their relationship in the environment of free sexuality then we can trust that two people have truly "found" each other. Once we no longer need to keep our wishes secret from each other, a new voyage in life can begin: truth in sexuality, truth in love, truth in partnership, truth instead of secrets, lies, and bad conscience. **Thereby a gate in the cellular system of the human being opens, which had been sealed by thousands of vows over generations.**

Free sexuality is not arbitrary promiscuity, it is not pornographic, nor is it indiscriminate group sex. Such fantasies emerge from the imaginations of people that do not have the possibility to fulfill their sexual wishes with dignity and solidarity.

Free sexuality is the encounter between people wanting to meet on the basis of contact and trust. Please reflect on this – contact and trust. It is not a matter of how many partners one has and is not about the savage survival of the fittest. It is about humanizing sex and love. It is appalling how the term "free sexuality" has been abused and falsified by the press. I know how difficult it is to bring this thought through. Actually it is no thought, but an offer from creation. It does not make much sense to argue about an experience one has not had.

Free sexuality can only fulfill its humane function when it follows social and ethical conditions given by a community of trust.

Most participants in our Love School courses realize within a few days how freely sexuality flows when they accept that they are actually **"allowed."** Free sexuality is a prerequisite for a free civilization. It is as integral to the culture of the upcoming era as free thinking and free religion. It should not be relegated to brothels or swinger clubs, for it belongs to life. This story illustrates the practice of free sexuality, as it happens in Tamera over and again: Two friends realize they desire the same man. One of them is in a relationship with this man. As night approaches the woman involved with the man senses the secret wish of the other to spend the night with her boyfriend. Without hesitation she offers her friend and her boyfriend her room. This kind of event is almost normal in the love life of Tamera. Through the culture of free sexuality a new ethic of solidarity emerges. When people hate or avoid each other because they desire the same person there is always war in the air. So long as the people involved believe their behavior to be normal, war cannot be prevented. In fact most people still believe it is okay to defeat their competitor. Such thoughts perhaps belong to the museums of anthropology, but certainly not to the ethics a reasonable human culture.

We live in a war society. We recognize in these examples how closely the question of war and peace is linked with apparently banal matters. There is a point in the relationship between the genders that determines whether there will be war or peace on Earth.

Free sexuality is not an ideology, nor a decision for or against monogamy or other forms of sexual expression. Free sexuality is simply the fulfillment of sexual wishes without lies or deceit, without humiliation or violence. A couple might just as freely decide for polygamy or for monogamy. In the experience of our community, the decision for a monogamous relationship is usually a temporary choice taken in order to experience enhanced intimacy. It is clear to all that this decision is respected and supported by the community.

Free sexuality is and was an essential factor in the stability of our community. It leads to relief within the within members of the group, for sex loses the demonic power it had when it was hidden. Through the convention of sexual suppression, the subconscious is teeming with dammed up sexual energies and fantasies. It is normal for people to be "over-sexed," chock full of covert or overt desires. When an average man encounters a beautiful woman he looks at her breasts and must make concerted efforts to disguise his thoughts. In a culture of free sexuality one acknowledges these things; one can laugh about them; no one has to hide their desire. Honesty in sexual matters allows for an historic cultural renewal. Through free sexuality the tide of trust and life joy rises.

The healing possibilities that would be accessible to the human being were the *"orgonotic current"* (see Glossary) of sexuality freely available to him has been described in the works of Wilhelm Reich.[4] Reich was a great pioneer for sexual truth; he opened gates to a completely new perspective on the origin and healing of disease, particularly in relation to cancer.[5] His vision can only find fulfillment in a life of liberated sexuality.

Sexuality is a superpower. Our attractions and repulsions, sexual signals and links, hopes and disappointments go through all of society like a nerve system, permeating every office, every shopping mall, every art exhibition, every conference, every group, every company, every political party. The healing of sexuality is perhaps the most revolutionary step in the present healing work after thousands of years of suppression and neglect. The sadomasochism that has spread in the underground of society signifies an attempt to break the borders and return to the body the freedom it lost in the narrow cage of bourgeois morality. For the sake of healing, this explosive inner power needs to be guided in a positive direction.

In the frame of free sexuality, the sexual powers that have thus far led to violence and destruction are no longer condemned, but transformed into the humane power of vital, sensual love. A new, humane culture is rooted in a new relation of the bodies.

The Mother from Auroville said that the revolution takes place in the body. What she referred to was the reception and integration of supramental energy into the cellular system. This also belongs to the vision of the new human being. We will see how these two directions of embodiment – the spiritual and the sexual – extend toward a common line of transformation.

Ethics of Free Sexuality

In order to live a humane and fulfilling life some guidelines to free sexuality need to be learned.

First: Sexual passion is not yet love. Sexual passion belongs to the stream of life and must therefore be freed from any hypocrisy. Sex is fully "allowed." It must be protected from any malice and defamation. But we need to remain honest. If we want sex we should not speak of love. Partnership cannot be established on the basis of sexual enthusiasm alone, for partnership is a personal relation and soul connection.

Second: Free sexuality requires "contact." Act only when contact and trust is established between you and the other. The thought that one can do anything within the context of free sexuality is a common misunderstanding. Yes, anything is allowed – when it happens in contact. This means heart opening and perception. Only then will both people sexually unite in a good way. Without contact they follow their own fantasies and do not find a common rhythm. Sexuality without contact easily leads to violence, and secret violent fantasies often steer sexual activity, leaving both people unfulfilled. Those who want fulfilling sex must learn to establish contact, for the principles of sexual ethics arise out of contact. For most people stepping into community, the first task consists of learning about contact – contact instead of projection, contact instead of masquerades, contact with and unconcealed joy for one another. This is what allows the sensitivity to one another to arise, leading the sexual play to its magical climax.

Third: If you desire someone sexually, consider whether the time is right. Are you really available for it? Is your heart free? If you feel in your heart chakra and in the solar plexus that you are free, then go for it! If you feel fear, then wait. Only go if you are confident that you can remain centered within yourself; that you can maintain your self-respect and that you do not lose yourself as you surrender. We refer to this quality of centeredness as the "blue sphere." (The term comes from the book *Traumsteine* [Dream Stones] by Sabine Lichtenfels. The teaching priestess tells her female students of the blue sphere and that it is important to always keep this sphere in one's own center when one approaches men with erotic wishes. She advises...

It is important that you feel and get to know this sphere. It shows you when the time is right to carry out the sexual act. When you lose perception of it, your sexuality will become unbalanced. It will drive you into insatiable desire and neediness.[6]

Fourth: When you have had a beautiful experience, give thanks for it and do not demand continuation. There is no right to possession in love. The continuation will come on its own if it is meant to.

Fifth: The question of whether we want to live monogamously or in polygamy, heterosexually, homosexually, bisexually, or any other arrangement is answered on the basis of our inner truth. It is not a contradiction to long for a partner and at the same time for erotic adventures with others. It only becomes betrayal when we deny our own truth in front of the other.

Sixth: If you experience temporary impotence do not be ashamed, but consider this humorous advice:

When someone is impotent he believes that he must be able to do something, which in reality one does not need to be able to do – and what one is especially able to do naturally when one no longer thinks whether one can or not. The assumption of having to be able to do what one in reality does not need to be able to do, because one can automatically do it if one no longer thinks about being able to do it or not, in most cases leads to disturbances in one's natural ability. Whoever is thus seriously unable, sees himself evermore affirmed in his wrong assumption of having to be able. This is how sex becomes a futile high-performance sport. If one is really unable and no longer has any land in sight, we want to ask him not to take it too seriously.[7]

There is always help when one lets go.

Chapter 21: Objective Ethics

How does trust arise among human beings? How does trust arise between man and woman, human being and animals, human being and nature, and between human being and the world at large? This question has been a central to our research since the very beginning of our project. Establishing trust is profoundly revolutionary in a society where disguises and lies have become necessary for survival. We need to thoroughly change our ways in order to be able to trust each other in the critical areas of sex, money, or power.

There is a universal objective ethic in the coexistence of the great family of life, the "legal code" of the Sacred Matrix. It is determined by the elementary interconnectedness and interdependence of all beings. Every thought that follows contains an ethical imperative: we human beings are the **eye of evolution** and we are entrusted to direct it **peacefully**. We live in a **community of life** with animals and plants. All creatures have the same right to life. All are all organs of the great organism of life; we therefore need to care for and support them all. Animals are our natural cooperation partners in the universal community of life. The fight between human being and animal thus comes to a definitive end. We do not torment animals; we support them in their development and joy of life.

Each nation, culture, and peoples, each tribe, group, and individual is an organ in the body of humankind. Organs must not hurt one another. We do not tolerate violence. We replace the thought of revenge with the thought of "grace" – mercy and forgiveness. We comply with the precepts of life, which we regard as non-negotiable. They apply to all places on our planet.

Establishing functioning projects and communities requires adherence to certain rules, without which no real trust can come into being. The founding canon of a nonviolent human culture certainly contains the following precepts of the objective ethics:

Truth
Mutual support
Responsible participation in the community
Transparency
Reliability
Care for the animal world

These words are easily read, but as soon as we look into them more closely we recognize that they are all keywords for a moral revolution. What does truth mean for example? What does it mean among love partners? Can man and woman tell the truth to one another without destroying their relationship? Do truth and couple relationship fit together? What does the woman do when she asks the man whether he also loves others and he says "yes"? And the other way around? Has not untruth for a long time been a condition for the survival of our love relationships? And furthermore what happens when a child speaks his fraction of the truth to his teacher, a student to his professor, an employee to his boss, or a member of parliament to his party? The society would explode. The lie has become a firm component of our culture, a prerequisite for its cohesion. This is why hardly anyone can any longer understand what is meant by truth. In a community of trust we speak of truth first and foremost in that way that a child speaks of it – that one simply does not lie. (Yet the issue of truth goes much deeper; see Chapter 24).

Let us take the next one: "mutual support." This sounds good. But how is it enacted in relationships, in marriages, in alleged friendships? Do partners support one another? Or do they engage in petty competitions and secret power games? Without the basis of unreserved trust there will not be a single functioning community, no permanent love relationship, no functioning social order, no sustainable economy. What kind of economy would come to being if we conducted our financial processes with truth, trust, and mutual support? These are questions in the research labs of the new centers. The success of the great work will depend on how they are answered. We immediately see that we need a new basis for our human relationships order to fulfill the precepts of the objective ethics.

These objective ethics are a universal fact. They exist in the structure of creation and inside every human being as our original conscience. Lusseyran, the French resistance fighter mentioned above, has described this in depth. This blind man had an inner screen which enabled him to correct his course. The screen showed to him the external world through the lens of his inner processes. In his book, *Against the Pollution of the I,* he writes…

> *When I was sad, when I was afraid, all shades became dark and all forms indistinct. When I was joyous and attentive, all pictures became light. Anger, remorse, plunged everything into darkness. A magnanimous resolution, a courageous decision, radiated a bright beam*

of light. By and by I learned to understand that love meant seeing and that hate was night. In this way I realized that morals (not social morals, but spiritual ones) were not merely a collection of abstract rules, but an ordered arrangement, an arrangement of facts as well as the ability to manage the light.[1]

While the objective ethics are the rules of a future human culture, they will not be perfectly adhered to anywhere immediately. We must take care that they do not become new grounds for moral censure or for generating bad conscience anew. Neither legislator nor judge will enforce them. It is rather that as people become autonomous they will understand and naturally abide by them.

Liberation from the Emotional Body

"Never act from emotional reactivity" is a principle of successful conflict resolution. We carry bulging emotional bodies. The smallest things, be it someone slightly clearing their throat or an ironic remark, can be the final straw. A society, which learned by necessity to suppress its emotions, generation after generation, lives under the threat of bursting, wherein the mass of suppressed collective emotion erupts into hate and violence. Our world is full of it. Most revolutions to date have derived more from the emotional body than from mental clarity. This is why they generated the historic *perpetuum mobile* of violence.

No solutions can arise in this way. Only those who are autonomous, free from the occupation of their emotional body, can find the higher level of order where the solutions lie.

Do not surrender to your emotional body; keep a clear mind; do not act from reactive emotion! This is basic advice for modern peace workers. The emotional body is part of our psychological anatomy; we cannot and we should not seek to remove it. Deep feelings such as love, compassion, and grief originate here. We must not suppress these feelings, on the contrary – we should open our hearts again. The pressing emotions such as anger, envy, or fear, also reside in the emotional body and will of course take over unless we have learned to stop them. Learning to control the tyranny of such reactivity, becoming the master in one's own house – this is what is meant by liberation from the emotional body.

It is a matter of developing "power." The teaching in all authentic spiritual traditions, from Jesus Christ to Prentice Mulford, Jacques Lusseyran to Peace Pilgrim, is about developing power. In order to cope with the challenges of our time, in order to be able to live a free life, we need the power to step out of emotional reflexes and follow new thoughts. He who faces a difficult task recognizes the imperative of establishing this power within him. People that want to take on a leading position in our turbulent times must be able to liberate themselves from their own emotional body and to make their decisions on the basis of higher wisdom – the wisdom of that universal intelligence which always guides us when we open ourselves for it.

This is a fundamental thought in the revolutionary healing theory: liberate yourself from the preoccupation with emotions and neediness, so you can become inwardly free for the spiritual powers of the universe to work through you. This is the source of happiness for the artist, the lover, and those who work for transformation. It is the joyful spirit that will unite the new communities.

Emotion and Mind

Translator's Note: Mind in this context refers to the German "Geist," which is more comprehensive than "mind" in English. It encompasses the mental and intellectual faculties as well as those of spirit and soul. Mind in that sense is the interface between intellect, spirit and soul and that which connects all of them. Mind is similarly used in Buddhist teachings.

Human autonomy begins with independent thinking. To be able to think independently we need to detach from our emotional body. So long as we are entangled with our emotions we cannot stand outside of events, and are therefore unable to think clearly. In this identified state we are part of the problem, not the solution. It is the mind that frees us from this prison. As soon as we mentally break through the state of identification, the process of insight and liberation begins. In order to be able to solve a problem we need a mental and spiritual point of view outside of the problem. We are in fact mentally and spiritually configured to take a standpoint outside of the problem. The mind is an "organ of insight." The less the forces of the emotional body besiege us, the more freely this organ can operate. It is the organ of the universal spirit or, as Teilhard de Chardin termed it, the "inner base station of God" in the human being.[2] As soon as we leave the fog of identification, we become the thinking organ and eye of evolution. We can recognize what evolution is doing and what it needs. We ourselves are agents of evolution. Humanity however has undertaken many things to eliminate this capacity. Independent thinking has long been punishable by death. In former times those who deviated from the doctrine of the church were executed, like Giordano Bruno, the sixteenth century Dominican monk who was a pioneering philosopher, mathematician, and astronomer, and who was burned at the stake. The fight against mind and spirit continues to this day. Many people in the alternative movement believed they should not follow the head, but the belly. In reality the opposite is the case. The emotional body sits in the belly; it follows the mind; the mind regulates the belly. We often have belly pain because the head is thinking wrongly. When we think in the right way, the belly calms. It is always mind and spirit that steer our organism including our emotions, both our well-being and depression. Mind and spirit therefore play a crucial role in the healing of the individual, as in the healing of the entire human race. Conscious or subconscious thoughts are the ones that steer our emotions. Thinking and theorizing holds a key function in the emancipation of society. The young revolutionaries of our time need a mental and spiritual education through which they become familiar with the faculties of thinking. The crucial mechanism of healing is put into motion when we start to think "properly" – a congruence of thinking and reality. Thinking resides on a high, emotion-free level on which mind and spirit calm because they harmonize with life. This allows the belly to rejoice as well as the heart. If we think this to the end we come to the commitment to "think in a way that love arises in our hearts."

Dealing with Supposed Enemies

Another criterion of successful peace work is stepping away from any kind of hostile thinking. A community that requires enemy stereotypes in order to maintain its inner cohesion still contains remnants of fascism. When a person is able to state sincerely and clearly, "I have no more enemies," then he is in a good state for peace work. It is a goal of modern character work to reach the psychological, mental, and spiritual maturity where all enemy stereotypes dissolve. Peace workers following the objective ethics do not fit into the structures of conventional society; they sometimes live in a hostile world where they are denounced and persecuted. This is why it is especially important for them to find a firm inner basis from which they can freely act without getting entangled in blind reactions.

In order to take a clear position toward opponents, all inner stirrings of fear and hostility need to disappear, for all "opponents" once lay in diapers, all have cried for their mothers, all have wept in heartache, all are afraid of condemnation, and enjoy friendliness. *"There are no enemies; there are only potential friends,"* writes Sabine

Lichtenfels.[3] Friendliness is a high virtue in dealing with opponents. We should also consider that each of today's opponents could have been a friend yesterday. Each of our friends today could have been an opponent yesterday. And each of today's opponents can be a friend tomorrow. Moreover, could it not be that you yourself have once been someone you would consider an enemy today? It is a high standard to see enemies as potential friends. Maintaining solidarity and authority in the tension of antagonism is part of the mental training for the new revolutionaries.

The distinction between friend and enemy is often rooted in our emotional body and is therefore not subject to serious discernment. To be free of fear of any opponent, one must be sure where one stands and have no skeletons in the closet. When we are sure of what we do and have neither fear nor bad conscience then the hostile world from which we needed to flee transforms into a world full of potential friends or colleagues.

We often judge a person simply because we are afraid of him or because we feel "seen through" by him. Most of what we criticize in others is that which we unconsciously reject or hate in ourselves. This is why "stop judging yourself" is an important guideline in dealing with alleged enemies. The more self-acceptance we are able to develop, the less we will judge others and the less we will think within this friend-enemy schema. There is no such distinct schema in the world; there is only a continuum of varying roles between the two. Tat tvam asi. People who redeem themselves from judgment will no longer judge others either, and thereby a human bridge forms that can allow miracles to happen. Jesus said, *"Do not judge so that you will not be judged."*[4] "Do not judge!" is the key phrase that will eventually also free us from our own fear. **Where there is no more fear, there also exists no more enmity.**

We all come from an endless series of perpetration and victimhood. The perpetrators became victims and vice versa; this is how it has gone on for thousands of years. We can only end this fatal chain by unconditionally stepping out of the system of revenge. This is of course difficult when we think of the mass murderers of our time, of the crimes in Chechnya, Syria, or Gaza – or when we, like our friends in San José de Apartadó (Colombia), stand face to face with the killers of our relatives. It does, however, become easier to step out of revenge when we look into the killers' biographies. Alice Miller has provided moving examples of the childhoods of people that committed horrific crimes later in life. My intention is not to therapeutically justify or excuse their actions, but to lead to a radical insight. If we could see how Hitler's father, Alois, beat his mother in front of his young eyes and continued by beating him, we would probably pause for a moment and briefly allow another feeling to rise, toward even one of the most horrible human beings of the last century.

We know how it is to be publically slandered and consequently to be thrown into powerless rage, which no longer allows for sensible action. At that time we did not yet know that there are mental and spiritual guidelines for such situations. Never act out of reactive emotions, for you only weaken yourself!

Behind all things there exists a higher guidance. Transform anger into power. Act in a way that peace arises within you! Hold your reaction until you have a peaceful attitude, thus the power to guide your next action will be with you. If the power is with you, hatred is extinguished. Maybe there is even a streak of love toward those that have afflicted you. Do not force yourself into any love however; do not violate your heart; simply renounce hatred!

Some years ago Sabine Lichtenfels led a peace pilgrimage in Israel-Palestine during which she visited an Israeli settlement in the occupied territories. The participants thereby were given an opportunity to transform their fear and hatred into compassion and reconciliation. She has described the astonishing events of this pilgrimage in her book, *Grace: Pilgrimage for a Future without War*. She writes...

I practiced and learned to see the Christ in every human being wherever I was and throughout the pilgrimage... I look for the core of the human being behind all the roles and masks of alienation. It is often difficult to be in this kind of presence... GRACE demands self-knowledge. And self-knowledge is not always easy. To discover flaws in others is much more pleasant and easy than to unmask oneself. Everything within me wants to cry out in anger and outrage when I sit opposite a young officer and listen to his excited explanations about the ideological values of his country. All of a sudden it occurs to me that he could just as well be my son and immediately I begin to see the human being behind his role.[5]

Chapter 22: What is Peace?

War is a serious disease of Homo sapiens – a real mental illness. When governments promote things that are designated for killing people, we can see that society is suffering from an inconceivable illness of consciousness. It has lost its moral competence. To the aphorism "it has always been this way," we ask, "is it wrong to correct a mistake because it has 'always' been this way?" War definitely has no place in the image of the future world.

We are living in a morphogenetic field of war. The power that lies in weaponry is tremendous. Many young men are fascinated by it. The peace society needs to develop a mighty alternative to counter the insanity of weaponry. What is this alternative? It is a new movement that spreads a potent morphogenetic field of an unconditional stand for all of life on Earth.

Peace is the power of life free from fear, connected to human solidarity. Peace is more than the opposite of war; peace is a quality of life that, during the past few thousand years, could not be manifested in a lasting way because the intra-human conditions were lacking. People fought for peace while filled with the war that had been carved into their hearts through a harsh history. Sabine Licthenfels writes...

> *Human beings have been praying for peace for millennia and they have fought for peace, but in their inner consciousness they have forgotten what peace is. They no longer know its inner laws. Human beings lack an encompassing inner vision of peace. A vision is an objective reality that can be seen and felt from within. It is inherent as a possibility in evolution and is waiting to be seen and accessed by human beings again.*[1]

This means that the vision for peace needs to be "recalled" from the cosmic database. It already exists there and it is our honorable task to cooperate with the universe and manifest this vision. It exists as an entelechy in the plan of creation and in the genetic information at the core of our cells. We can physically feel whether a vision is right or wrong. If we act in accordance with true peace a healing power instantaneously arises in our organism. Peace Pilgrim, who walked with an unshakable commitment to ending war said, *"There is a criterion by which you can judge whether the thoughts you are thinking and the things you are doing are right for you. That criterion is: have they brought you inner peace? If they have not, there is something wrong with them – so keep trying."[2]*

It is easy to read this sentence if one does not take it seriously. It contains probably the deepest answer to the question of how we ourselves can generate peace – by acting in a way that it arises within us! If we try to follow this advice for only one day we will soon recognize that we are constantly making mistakes. This discovery can change one's life. We ourselves generate turbulence through the thoughts we are thinking, through speaking inconsiderate words, and through our unrestrained reactions to inconvenient situations. However we are "normally" not sufficiently awake to recognize this inner war. We do not live in a state of witnessing ourselves. But this is exactly what we need to do in order to understand the dimension of Peace Pilgrim's words. What is peace? Peace is the life of human beings that have entered into this witnessing state. They will no longer hate anyone. Peace is the unconditional, mutual acceptance of people that trust one another because they have perceived one another.

In this context, we gain a new understanding of the notion that we can only generate as much peace on the outside as we have reached within ourselves. Of course there are external economic and political factors that are beyond our reach and which continue to generate collective war. I have already discussed how global peace cannot be established so long as the economic and political conditions, which constantly produce war, persist. However, in order to be able to effectively counter the external conflicts, we need the inner power of peace as described by Peace Pilgrim. Only if we are equipped with this power will we be able, step-by-step, to pierce the outer structures and change the entire system. The way is from inside out.

Whether we are able and willing to flip our inner switch toward peace is of crucial therapeutic and social significance. The power of our vision depends on the extent to which peace has already manifested within us. We can only believe in outer peace if we have established a firm peace power within. One needs to be very strong in order to act in ways that generate internal peace within conflict situations. This requires complete mastery over our reactive emotions. In order to fulfill Peace Pilgrim's criterion we need to shift from ego-centeredness to service for a higher purpose. If I work only for myself I permit myself small inner imprecisions. If I work for a greater purpose, a professionalism develops within me; I become focused and precise because my purpose demands it. This psychological system change protects us from the attacks of our own emotional body. Aside from this, it is advisable to prevent avoidable mistakes and to be guided by truth, for inner war is often connected to untruth and to the fear of being found out. **Only freedom from a bad conscience enables us to be liberated from the latent fear of being found out and judged. Those who are free of a bad conscience do not fear external judgment.** It is often very simple details on the smallest scale that determine the large-scale situation.

Lasting peace can only arise in a community of people that have completely overcome the old concept of attack and defense through no longer being anchored in their ego, but on a higher level of order. This change is key to the current transformation. If a group succeeds in building a coherent morphogenetic field of peace then a strong psychological power grows, for true peace is connected with the powers of the *Sacred Matrix*. From such a connection, we can send healing powers to endangered projects in the crisis areas of our planet. When peace projects are connected to the Sacred Matrix, **peace workers are under great protection**; they can "no longer be hurt psychologically."[3]

In summer 2014, we experienced how a new war was created in Israel-Palestine. What happened there was like a last unconscious rise of the old field of war. The spirit of revenge dominated the field there. It was the archetype of the devil, which heated up the same psychological structures of hatred and murderousness on both sides – in the Israeli Knesset and in Hamas. Left unchecked these structures operated all the way to the (secretly desired) genocide. Bombing Gaza was an act of human cruelty that could only cause tears, pain, and despair in all open hearts. We see the same in Syria and in the "Islamic State." They do everything to stir up the emotional body; they are extremists that carry their will for evil, for destruction, and revenge to the very end.

What can we do? What can the new peace groups do? It is difficult to give a definitive answer. As a first action in the name of peace, people simply call out to each other to no longer participate, to no longer abide war service, to no longer follow the slogans of the warring parties, but to use their communication systems to wake as many people as possible from the war hypnosis. This first step requires courage and determination. It is easier to take it when the next step can already be seen – building new centers on behalf of Terra Nova. The groups that come together in the Middle East should know that they are not alone if they decide for a path of radical peace work. They are part of the newly developing planetary community. They should get in touch with Tamera and the other Terra Nova School groups.

PART IV
THE GLOBAL HEALING BIOTOPES PLAN

To enable a future without war we need convincing models. The models need to provide solutions for both the outer global crises and the crises of the inner human world. It is the inner human processes that determine the success or failure of our peace work. Human society needs to be newly anchored in the universal powers of life and creation (the Sacred Matrix) if it is to find the resolution that is needed. We need new models of living wherein truth, love, and solidarity become possible again. We need community in which the latent war between the genders has ended, in which free sexuality is based on truth and trust, and in which our fellow beings are respected as cooperation partners within a sacred alliance. We need intimate cooperation with nature and the universe because healing is the reconnection with the original power field of the divine world. This applies to the individual organism, to the organism of a community, and to the organism of all humankind.

The first step of this global work consists of creating Healing Biotopes. The second step entails connecting the Healing Biotopes in a global network. The third step is global field-building, which is no longer carried out by humanity, but by the laws inherent to the universal holon. This "morphogenetic world process" is described in the last part of this section.

Chapter 23: What is a Healing Biotope?

The Tamera peace research center in Portugal has been working on the global Healing Biotopes plan for two decades. It is a cultural idea for an era free of war and violence. A Healing Biotope is a community in which all beings involved – human beings, animals, plants, and waters – live together in a way that serves their mutual healing and development. It is crucial that there is trust among all those involved, for trust is the basis of healing. A new objective thus comes into play, one that has not yet been featured in ecological or economic questions – the strategic building of trust. This will require the overcoming of an historic barrier; most beings carry a deep conditioning of mistrust as a result of the historic trauma. **In order to generate trust, the barriers of fear, disguise, and deceit must be overcome.** The students and participants in a healing biotope know that they step into an innovative experiment, particularly in the Love School where they are confronted with new opportunities for their psychological and sexual development. The research is about new forms of communication and cooperation among human beings, as well as between human beings and nature. Gradually invisible beings are also integrated into the cooperation, for the world we are able to see is only the surface of the totality of all living beings. In every moment of our healing work multitudes of invisible helpers stand by our side. Esoteric terms such as "*deva* (see Glossary)," "guardian spirit," or "angel" connote a spiritual realm that could, little by little, be included in the conceptual planning of the new projects.

Healing Biotopes orient their work according to the truths of life. They are organized in such a way that life is able to carry out healing. We do this through new social, ecological and technical structures and through new forms of coexistence that align with the precepts of universal ethics. The greater the stability of these structures, the more intensively the healing process will act in all those involved.

The global Healing Biotopes project contains and manifests the principles and paradigms that, insofar as we know, will foster the humane habitation of all continents. Of course Healing Biotopes will take shape according to the cultural, geographic and climatic conditions of the countries they are in, but the core principles of creating a new culture will be the same everywhere. The project is not focused on one specific problem, such as famine, but on all problems for they all are inseparably related. The Hunger Project, which aimed to free the world from famine in the 1990s, could not succeed because the global practices of economic and political exploitation continued and continue to perpetuate hunger. The ending of worldwide hunger evidently necessitates the removal of the economic structures that generate it. This applies to any real humane renewal – it can only succeed on the basis of a new social, economic, and political order. There can be no humane world without revolution. However it is not a revolution through violence that is needed, but a revolution through insight and the application of the power inherent to our Christ nature: Revolution through taking a determined, non-negotiable stand for life.

The Healing Biotopes project aims for the healing of humankind and the Earth. In other words, it is about a finding a new direction for human evolution and about a new matrix for inhabiting our planet. Within this vast frame we have identified some focal points, the healing of erotic love for example, raising children, developing decentralized energy technologies, and the healing of water because these are key to our existence. The way in which humankind deals with water, which energy sources we use, and how we solve "issue number one" will essentially determine whether there will be peace or war on Earth.

The Primordial Cell for a New Planetary Culture

The concept of the Healing Biotope originated with the idea that there must be a structure – we called it the "cultural crystal" – that initiates a process of self-replication, much like a biological cell, once the structure is sufficiently developed and complex. This cultural crystal would be a universal structure applicable to all peoples and continents. In other words, the image of a Healing Biotope came from an intention to create a morphogenetic field for a new humane world. Evolution moves forward through creating morphogenetic fields (see Chapter 30).

Today we live in a morphogenetic field of war. From economic and political decisions to the processes in love relationships, a morphogenetic field of war characterizes this society, despite all moral efforts of individuals. We need to transform it into a morphogenetic field of peace. The civilization of the future is evolving from a morphogenetic field of peace. Resonance instead of violence, cooperation instead of competition, forgiveness instead of revenge – these are some of the characteristics of the new morphogenetic field.

For building the morphogenetic field an image crystalized and slowly solidified: the image of a "Healing Biotope." The Healing Biotope serves as the "primordial cell" of a new culture in the organism

148

of humankind. In this primordial cell, the focus and parameters need to be set relatively accurately to enable the cell to properly spread through the growing organism of the new planetary community. The global Healing Biotopes plan relies on the establishment of a first of these primordial cells that, with the help of a global network, will give rise to other such cells. A "morphogenetic condensation" is to be achieved in the noosphere, (the informational body of humankind), in which, bit by bit, variations on the original cell will crystallize. That which happened four billion years ago with the evolution of the first biological cell could happen in contemporary social evolution with the multiplication of the primordial planetary cell through morphogenetic field-building. (This process, which is described so linearly here, is in reality an historic process involving many projects and groups.)

The primordial cell contains the fundamental information matrix, the "DNA" of the new civilization. It gathers the most diverse forms of life and thereby brings forth new connection points, new synergies, new energy lines, and new directions of meaning, leading to new directions of growth. From the work of ants and spiders, bees and swallows, to the activities of children, of domestic animals, from water lilies in ponds and fruit trees in the Permaculture gardens, from the actions of craftsmen, technicians, excavator drivers, scientists, and priestesses, all the way to the workings of natural spirits, there develops a growing system of ever increasing coherence. **The greater the coherence, the more powerful the system and its capacity for growth – it seems increasingly to develop "by itself."** The most astonishing phenomenon we perceived in the difficult times of our project was when no solution was obvious to us and new faculties of creativity and self-organization arose within the community that helped us to find a way out.

An essential condition for the development of the primordial cell is the coherence between its composite working areas. In Tamera we coined the term "coherent information system" (CIS) as a reminder to attend to this coherence. CIS was and is a central thought in the implementation of the new centers. In a Healing Biotope all subprojects need to be intellectually and spiritually compatible, this means that they need share basic principles and goal-orientation. The informational matrix for raising children for example should match the core information of the Love School, the political education, the nutrition, technology, ecology et cetera. Where this is found, we have a highly robust coherent information system. **The stability of a system depends on its coherence with the Sacred Matrix and on the coherence within and between its subsystems (working areas or subprojects).**

The principle of the coherent information system brings with it a high moral responsibility. How much secret cheating can we tolerate if we seriously want to create a world of peace? How many industrially-produced consumer goods can one still use knowing the barbaric ways in which they were made and distributed? Can one still drink canned milk or eat chocolate produced by Nestle? These are serious questions in a coherent community. They concern the issue of complicity. When thinking about complicity we should not restrict our attention to questions of consumption for we are also complicit when we participate in the destructive ways of thinking and the subliminal emotions of conventional society. Questions of complicity must not be suppressed and nor should they be allowed to escalate to moral fanaticism or be used as excuses to tyrannize each other, for they are meant to serve peace and love. The cultivation of the primordial cell is a community undertaking. It develops out of the complex relationships within a community and the relationships which that group has established with the global network. The Tamera community engages in continuous communication with individuals and groups all over the world in order to fine-tune the project so that it can reach "morphogenetic maturity." To this end the aspects of Eros, religion, and economy need to be developed further.

Chapter 24: Creating Functioning Communities

It is not the private interests that create lasting fellowship among men, but rather the goals of humanity.[1]

~ *I Ching*

The natural human being is, as is probably every living being, a communitarian being. Everything that people need can be found in a healthy community, particularly the ethical and spiritual qualities of life. Historically the human soul lost its anchor through the collapse of community. The attempt to reestablish human community is therefore an experiment of historic relevance, which also brings us into contact with the global trauma that we have internalized. This is why most attempts thus far have failed. It may be that nothing is more difficult than creating functioning communities yet it is precisely this that is the task of our time. The biologist Lynn Margulis says, ***"If we are to survive the ecological and social crisis we have caused, we may be forced into dramatically new kinds of cooperative ventures."***[2] That which seemed to be a romantic adventure around the times of Monte Verita in the early twentieth century, to the hippy times in the sixties, that which we dreamt of around evening campfires, has become pivotal to the future of human civilization: how do we establish real community?

Community is not just a sentimental dream of young people, but the next stage of evolution; the people of the future will live in community. Thousands of communities have been founded since the 1970's, but hardly any have survived. The longing for community, which brought people together, failed due to inner and interpersonal conflicts. The inability to resolve "issue number one" led frequently to social turbulence which ultimately brought groups to collapse. The building of a functioning community requires an intellectual and spiritual foundation as well as very determined people who know what they are doing. By entering into community we make a complete system change from a private to a communitarian biography – a shift of our inner assemblage point. We step into a new life, a new ethic, and a new basis for processing our eternally unresolved conflicts revolving around sex, love and partnership. Community is an historic issue, which concerns the reconditioning of the inner human world. **No one** living in a functioning community will breakdown from jealousy or heartache, for they have another anchor in life.

The necessity of habitual dissemblance becomes redundant in functioning community. Disguise, lies, and deceit no longer make any sense in a community dedicated to the well-being of all. When people no longer need to disguise themselves in front of one another they will recognize and support each other. Human will recognize human. Man will recognize woman and woman will recognize man. As stated in the previous section, truth, fidelity, mutual support, and taking responsibility for the whole are basic characteristics of communitarian ethics. We can recognize the new humans by the reliability with which they maintain these disciplines. Disguise, lies, and deceit no longer make any sense in a community dedicated to the well- being of all. Trust gives the power to break through old barriers; when we defuse interpersonal minefields, the roots of fear and violence disappear from the psychological underground. The future without war begins with the first functioning community.

"Community" – an easy word and a complex issue. It is not actually more difficult than establishing a functioning company, though. The only difference is that there is already a morphogenetic field for setting up a company, whereas there is as yet none for building a functioning community. This still needs to be created; it is key to the success or failure of the entire peace movement. The answer to the question as to how the wish for a variety of lovers becomes compatible with the longing for partnership with **one** person comprises part of the morphogenetic field of a functioning community. This answer, which we all need and which the world needs, will not come about on a psychological or therapeutic level, but from a new integration of human life into the universal order of community.

To establish resilient human relationships capable of enduring the inevitable conflicts, we need a profound basis of **truth.** What is truth? Certainly truth means that one does not lie. As we have seen, this is already quite a demand. But truth goes even further and deeper; truth is the congruence of my words and thoughts with what is really happening **within me.** Here lies the challenge. When a group debates an issue, the design of a basin for a spring for example, different opinions can collide. Misunderstandings and accusations might arise, with emotions ranging from aggression all the way to open anger. If one looks into what is actually happening one sees the extent to which the undigested inner problems of those involved – the subconscious Oedipus complexes, authority conflicts or power struggles – are at work. Arguments ostensibly about subject matter are actually driven by

152

psychological and interpersonal conflicts. One group member refutes another vociferously only because last night the latter kissed the woman that the former would himself have liked to have kissed. Many talks fail due to the entanglement of subject matter and ego problems. I have witnessed a person asserting that water is hurt when it is captured in a stone basin. In reality the pain was clearly not on the side of the water, but within the person. Subjective processes are suppressed when they are projected into the objective world. Every "normal" colleague would be indignant if we were to tell him that his assertion actually refers to his own problem and not to the water's problem. However, for the creation of a community of trust conflicts such as these need to be seen through and resolved. It was for this purpose that we introduced the SD Forum (see Chapter 19) in which, with the agreement of the whole group, one is allowed to speak the full truth. Forum is facilitated by people who have recognized, to a considerable extent, the working of these processes in themselves and are ready and able to speak the truth. Whenever self-disclosure occurs without judgment, the group experiences something new in terms of truth. For many this is a very moving, even overwhelming experience. A community intending to collaborate over a long period relies on this kind of psychological cleansing. It reveals a deeper level of truth, which has to do with self-knowledge. It is only on this level that true communication among human beings can begin.

There will be no humane world without resilient communities. When I was offered a professorship forty years ago I declined in obedience to the inner advice to establish a community that really works. It turned out to be an adventurous and very painful process. I had been quite an individualist and was not particularly disposed to make the issue of community the priority in my life. I needed to retreat to a hermitage in the Bavarian Forest for a half year to make this decision.

The first step was to begin a group and to introduce free sexuality. The participants were not prepared for this so it made for a shocking beginning. After about five years however, it was matter of course. It was like a small miracle. The change from couple relationship to free sexuality occurred as if by itself. No one was forced; hardly anyone fought the idea. **It happened "by itself" in the way all things integrated in the higher spiritual power field happen by themselves.** Today, looking back, I am astonished by how all the essential steps in the development of the project have, more or less, unfolded by themselves: the development of self-revelation (SD) in the group, the spreading popularity of painting, the transition from private to communitarian thinking, the new management of water, the skills to survive in Spartan conditions, mutual financial support in emergency situations, the creation of a sanctuary for mistreated animals from the neighborhood, cooperation with government agencies, communication with natural spirits and so on. All of this somehow came "by itself" without enforcement, without battles, without the usual power struggles and competition. I recognized that from the idea of community a program unfolded as if by itself. **The plan of creation seemed to contain an immanent concept, which we recalled by entering the keyword "community" and which guided our steps from then on.**

On this path we encountered a virtual entity, the original matrix of community that exists in the implicate order of creation. We called it the *prehistoric utopia*. The idea that there was a primordial cosmic pattern for human community, applicable to all peoples, was fascinating. It also opened a new gate for us. Through the psychic abilities of my partner, Sabine Lichtenfels, we came to concrete visions for implementing the global Healing Biotopes plan. We understood how desperately the disregarded fellow inhabitants of our property, the animals, tiny creatures, and invisible spirits, need to be integrated into the work. Everywhere that we start a garden and build houses we encounter small co-creatures such as snails, worms, beetles, which along with us generate a positive or negative energy field. A functioning community pays attention to establishing a good living environment together with all fellow creatures, small and big. Eike Braunroth, creator of the peace gardens, demonstrated through his research the extent to which all of our fellow beings, even the smallest ones, seek human advice and abide by it.[3] Even the snails follow advice about which parts of the garden are reserved for them and which they should leave alone. Unfortunately his pioneering work has not yet entered public consciousness. It needs to be integrated by the new centers. We have allocated a research area, which we humorously call the "Metaphysical Hectare" for this area of study (see Chapter 25).

Over the years one gets to know the particular relevance of certain animals or plants as energy and information carriers within the system. Questions of animal husbandry, even of meat consumption, then appear in ever new contexts. After four years of keeping fish we remain unwilling to catch a single one to eat. This is the kind of difficulty we find in things that we would previously have carried out habitually. We are in development and are far from finished. We advise all newly forming groups to refrain from taking fundamental decisions prematurely and from adopting dogmas that easily lead to fanaticism and intolerance. The topics that need attention are often so complex

154

that it is not possible to come to quick answers. Life is constantly revealing itself to us. *"First it comes always differently, and second never as you think."*[4]

Prehistoric Utopia

The prehistoric utopia is the universal timeless model of human community and society – its universal pattern or its original matrix. In our project a special area of research, guided by Sabine Lichtenfels, is the investigation into the cultures and vestiges of prehistoric peoples through for example the temples on Malta and Gozo (see her books *Traumsteine*[5] [*Dream Stones*] and *Temple of Love*[6]) and the well-preserved stone circle of Almendres near Évora in Portugal. In collaboration with the geomancer Marko Pogačnik, Sabine Lichtenfels discovered and described the pattern of this stone circle and received a series of astonishing messages. She writes…

This information also slumbers as primordial experience in all human beings living now. Here lies your origin, from which you yourself emerge and which you have all forgotten. This memory was and is systematically assailed, for it is the seed for creating new, nonviolent cultures. This is not at all wanted by those presently in power. Here lies the code for a possible future, which has long been sleeping in your cells as information and dream. Today the Earth is dominated by an informational matrix that systematically deactivates such impulses. This is why it is so difficult to bore one's way to this memory.[7]

We soon recognized that the systems recorded here were beyond the knowledge of our sociologists or psychoanalysts. We were obviously dealing with a far more comprehensive form of human society than our own, one deeply anchored in the overarching order of Earth, nature, and cosmos; of incarnated and non-incarnated forms of life. The stone circle of Almendres arose in the fifth and fourth millennia BCE. According to the research conducted by Sabine Lichtenfels we have reason to believe that this was a time when human and animal were not afraid of one another for they belonged to the same family of life, they communicated with one another and therefore had no impulse to kill each other. The creators of the stone circle were in touch with cosmic and invisible realms. The sociology of this culture is a matter pure mystery science. The appearance of an eagle or a

1

snake, where a swarm of bees settles, where ants make their pathways and rats their subterranean cities has particular meanings. We have learned a great deal and continue learning. As we recall this original knowledge, we break fresh ground for a new cohabitation on our planet.

I do not think that all new centers need to start with this kind of mystery knowledge, but I assume that they will all enter this continent of consciousness once they have become attentive to the mysteries of life, once their inhabitants open their hearts and learn to trust. **It is not only small communities - all of humanity is on the way to realizing the prehistoric utopia. This is not a return to the past but the awakening to a prehistoric knowledge, which lies as a legacy in our cells and awaits manifestation in our time.**

Wolf-Dieter Storl, the inspired Austrian nature researcher, has immersed himself deeply in the mysteries of nature and into ancient ways of experiencing it. He has described the prehistoric utopia from his own experience. Storl offers insights into the mysteries of healing which were known to our ancestors and are carried into our time by authentic shamans.[8] The "medicine men" of the original native tribes are shamans; they possess "medicine," a supernatural, numinous faculty that enables them to heal others. Herbal medicine also contains secrets that will lead us to a new understanding of the prehistoric utopia. These relate directly to the inner connections between humans and the beings of nature, which have been lost in our culture; we need to see just how relevant this is to contemporary society. Even if not all of us can step into the animistic realm we can acknowledge the message it carries – that we live in a world of soul in which everything is in mysterious resonance. This applies even to the smallest of daily affairs. If when I walk through a meadow and step on the flowers, am I aware that bees need these flowers and that we need the bees because if they perish so too will we?

The Autonomous Individual and Grassroots Democracy

A functioning community needs independent human beings, not opportunist followers. The term community still carries the bad reputation of conformity, of "leveling down," and collectivism. The wish to belong to a community leads many people to renounce their own opinion and conscience in order to secure acceptance by the group. ⟩ not dare to object when authority figures make wrong ⟩. This is the situation within political parties, criminal gangs, ⟩st mass movements. In the dark times of history the law of community-building was "collectivism over individuality" and this still broadly applies within the parliaments of Western "democracies" today.

Community and the individual need not contradict one another; they complement one another. It is as a grave error to think that developing a community must be at the expense of the free individual. Exactly the opposite is true. A functioning community needs people that think independently. Only then can a strong communitarian self develop. Functioning community is based on trust. So long as the participants are the mouthpieces of a guru they cannot trust one another because they do not get to know each other. Trust among human beings is based not only on an emotional, but also on intellectual, spiritual, and ethical ground. The truth and autonomy of individual participants contributes to this intellectual and spiritual basis. Each human being has his own essential qualities. The community can only function humanely when it accepts and supports the distinctiveness of its individual participants. Then, the communitarian "super-self" can arise, which supersedes individual competence.

To get a healthy community off the ground the participants need to free themselves from the hypnotic spell of normality and to become the person they "actually" are. There is a profound difference between the "actual" (authentic, entelechial) human being and the role someone plays in order to cope with the conflicts of his existence. Everyone has – consciously or unconsciously – adopted a mask to ensure his or her own survival under the conditions of the globalized lie. On entering community this role is challenged until it can fully be deconstructed. This kind of self-revelation and transparency is a prerequisite for developing an emancipatory community, for people can only trust one another when they meet without masks. The individual must learn to become "himself" in order to become a member of a true human community. Those who enter a community make an existential decision; the change from an independent to a communitarian identity is profound. We are only at the beginning of communitarian development; it will fundamentally change the society of the future from the ground up.

There has been a lot of debate about grassroots democracy since the students' movement in the last century. Grassroots democracy was an anti-authoritarian counter to the patterns of leadership in conventional society. It set out to dissolve authoritarian structures; all group members were to be granted the same rights of participation. While the psychological underground of the participants was still dominated by competition and authority struggles, the result was mostly hopeless chaos. Humanity needs to develop the capacity for democracy and this requires the transformation of the inner world. The adoption of grassroots democracy is appropriate when all participants are able to take on responsibility for the group. This requires people that follow their conscience and are ready to place the common interest above their own. When this is in place grassroots democracy develops naturally as a basic form of living and working together. In the event that a group member does not agree with the established consensus and provides genuine arguments, the group will confer until that member can agree or until the decision is corrected. Sometimes this prolongs the decision-making process but it also bolsters the basis of trust within the group.

So we see that autonomous individuals, capable of placing the common interest above their own are necessary to both functioning communities and to grassroots democracy. These are people able to participate in decision-making processes through their own thinking; they do not subordinate themselves to any given ideology, public opinion, or mainstream belief. To date people such as these have been rare. In the Marxist movement one had to say what Marx said. In Pune one had to say what Bhagwan said. At Friedrichshof one had to say what Otto Muehl said. In the Christian Democratic Union (the German conservative political party) one must think as Angela Merkel thinks and in intellectual circles it is commendable to mimic the thoughts of *Der Spiegel* magazine. This is the collectivist structure of the old era, in which no autonomous human beings, no reliable partners arise, only followers whose judgment is barely reliable. It was less the fault of the gurus than the followers' longing for contact and togetherness that moved them to give up on their own thinking. Grassroots democracy cannot arise in this way; only unreflective collectivism. The anti-authoritarian movement arose in reaction to this mindless following and it threw out all the babies with the bathwater in its wholesale rejection of organized leadership. However the fact of the matter is that there are natural authority figures in every community. These are people trusted by others and/or those who distinguish themselves through special expertise. It is to be expected that their contributions will also carry a particular weight in grassroots democracy.

The turmoil around the issue of grassroots democracy fades away as soon as we integrate the inner world into the work and people begin to be authentic in a circle of trust and solidarity. It is self-evident that one listens to the thoughts and arguments of others when one trusts them. If they are wrong, one simply tells them so. When the others are

158

right, one corrects one's own thoughts. I appeal to every young person: turn away from hypnoses and ideologies. Be who you are!

Why We Did Not Fall Apart Due to the Usual Conflicts

Sally Silverstone, a woman from the core group of the celebrated but thwarted Biosphere II project in Arizona (in the early 1990s), asked us why we had not fallen apart as a result of the usual group conflicts. What power has kept the Tamera community together? As described above, **the establishment of transparency is indispensable to the cohesion of a group.** The most important processes in the hot areas of sex, money, and power need to be brought into transparency. A group that wants to survive should agree on establishing this early on. It has to be decided by the group; it does not just arise on its own. Left to our own devices we only repeat the familiar forms of dissimulation and opaqueness. **Transparency serves truth and trust.** Perhaps this sounds banal; in reality it allows highly advanced human coexistence. To establish transparency we developed the aforementioned SD Forum. Whenever a group member has a personal issue he can come into the middle of the circle and make visible his concern as directly and vitally as possible. Those bearing witness have the task to follow attentively and possibly to give comments. Through this a new social consciousness came into being. One no longer judges another harshly when one has really seen him. Sympathy slowly grows, even among people who would otherwise have not perceived or even fought against one another. "To be seen is to be loved" was the maxim we deduced from our experiences of the SD forums. In this community milieu theater and art developed. These are opportunities for liberating ourselves from identification with the role of victim and for placing ourselves as actors in the play of life, which we ourselves produce from moment to moment.

From the early days of the project there were people who had a great vision of community that enabled them to stay on track during all the struggles. Bit by bit a field of trust develops around people such as these; they are beneficial for every community. The participants of a community need to share a high goal to be willing and able to realize truth and trust. Those who consciously participate in building a community will very soon reach the threshold of a critical decision as to whether to follow the principles of the "objective ethics." Even if the social positioning of the participants is not clear, it should be agreed that everyone will adhere to the guidelines of the objective ethics. These are the rules of the Sacred Matrix.

Here we come to an important point in answer to Sally Silverstone's question. We have, as far as possible, followed the rules of the Sacred Matrix and have thereby integrated ourselves within a higher system of life. **A community following the behavioral guidelines of the Sacred Matrix (known intuitively by us all) is spiritually protected.** It is critical to the survival of those communities directly confronted by paramilitary forces or other criminals, as for example groups in the Middle East, Colombia, Brazil, and Mexico that they stand firm in the objective ethics. People committed to do this build strong trust among one another. This gives rise to an almost invincible power. We know how difficult it is for many groups to stay with the ethical guidelines under the trying conditions they face. They will succeed when their decisions are guided by the unifying field of a new planetary community.

Lastly I want to recall an aspect without which, in the long run, no community can stay together: **the spiritual magnetic field**. The group must know what it wants. It needs to have a mental and spiritual image, a concept that gives orientation to its work. From the beginning our project's founding team had an ambitious image of the community of life in the Healing Biotope. Most of the participants were not yet familiar with this image so conflicts arose; quite a few people got angry and left the project. Conflict is inevitable, but it dissolves when the truth underlying the struggle prevails. One example of this in our case was the truth of free sexuality. There are indisputable realities that need to be accepted for permanent coexistence to be possible. It has been clear to us since the outset that love needs to be freed from malice, that we need to step into a new, nonviolent relation to animals and that we need a new system for water, food, and energy. Even though we lacked clarity at times, we knew our goal and could distinguish between the powers that were serving life and those destroying it. All members of a community should agree on taking a stand for life! Once this thought had crystallized we had a basis for staying together. Last but not least, as soon as free sexuality works, there is a joy of life and truth at the foundation of community, which cannot be gained in any other way.

Chapter 25: The Sacred Alliance of Life

Evolution works toward convergence – toward the one. In the global consciousness of the new time the reintegration of all life into the "sacred alliance" takes place. If we understand that all beings are organs within the body of the great family of life, the next steps unfold naturally. This belongs to the new gospel. The family of life is healthy when its organs are healthy. The organs are healthy when they connect within the universal frequency of life. It is the energy of trust. The prophecy of Isaiah is, in principle, true! It says…

And the wolf will dwell with the lamb,
And the leopard will lie down with the young goat,
And the calf and the young lion and the fatling together;
And a little boy will lead them.
Also the cow and the bear will graze,
Their young will lie down together,
And the lion will eat straw like the ox.
The nursing child will play by the hole of the cobra,
And the weaned child will put his hand on the viper's den.
They will not hurt or destroy in all My holy mountain,
For the earth will be full of the knowledge of the LORD,
As the waters cover the sea.[1]

This astonishing vision from the seventh century BCE is affirmed by our experiences of animals' joy in their contact with people in Tamera. As mentioned above, we have a number of photographs that capture our hearts – lions embracing their guard on his return to them, a python that allows its head to be brushed by a baby, among others. In this original matrix, no violence exists.

Human beings are the eyes of evolution; we can perceive the interconnections and correlations within the biosphere and how its parts have become separate from one another. As we see this we also know how the parts can come together again. This is key to all that we do. When someone asks what the beating heart of Terra Nova is, we can answer that it is the sacred alliance of all living beings. When we speak of the new planetary community, we mean the sacred alliance of all beings, including humankind. As soon as peace arises where there has so far been fear we will recognize the service that those animals which we had expelled from our lives render to us – the snakes, rats, toads, and so-called garden "pests." We will weep when we recognize how we have behaved toward these animals and when we sense how they have always sought contact with us. We believed them to be vermin and still they approached us because they require our cooperation in the great plan of creation.

At present there are probably not many people on Earth who retain this primordial connection with life and its beings yet there are lots who can return to this state, for we all carry the image of the sacred alliance in our "meta-consciousness." At our current state of development, meta-consciousness is not in our awareness but is can become so, for it is built into our genetic structure. Meta-consciousness contains universal knowledge (*Akashic Records* – see Glossary), which is reflected holographically within the human being. Thus it follows that if a group of people establishes a new social order in accordance with the Sacred Alliance, they activate the image of an existence that is latent in everyone. The image can then be received everywhere and can therefore be manifested everywhere.

A sick child can become well when his small dog lies at his side. Every contact where closed hearts can open again is healing. When we tune into this we find ourselves in realms seldom spoken of because we are embarrassed by the feelings that arise. I ask all readers to open your hearts and to voice your feelings in clear, direct, and sober language. Finding authentic language for our feelings gives us access to truth. Wilhelm Reich has found an interesting definition for truth. *"Truth is full, immediate contact between the Living that perceives and Life that is perceived."*[2]

As every creature within the sacred alliance is an organ of the whole, all help to keep the whole intact and running. When there is a disturbance in one organ, all others need to engage in overcoming the disturbance. There are indications that certain co-creatures, whales and dolphins for example, have assumed the task to assist humanity it its survival mission.[3] From our observations in Tamera, we recognize a similarly supportive function in rats. The closer we look, the more fellow beings reveal themselves as helpers. Bees, for example, play a major part in agriculture; we would struggle to survive without them. In light of how highly complex and finely attuned the biospheric system is, it becomes urgently necessary to radically rethink our relation to animals.

There are many ways to reciprocate our fellow being's generosity in the spirit of loving and trustful cooperation. When, in the wake of an enlightenment experience, the Indian emperor Ashoka (around 200 BCE) turned away from warfare, he built thousands of water holes and hospitals for animals all over India. Creating animal sanctuaries for sick and injured animals contributes to building the morphogenetic field of the sacred alliance. As mentioned above, Eike Braunroth's peace gardens[4] offer incredible and more current examples of collaboration with so-called pests in the garden. In Tamera an amicable agreement with wild boars has developed; the boars generally adhere to the boundaries we set so we have no need to fence in our gardens.

Tamera's Metaphysical Hectare is a wild garden in which we research into the perception of and cooperation with all visible and invisible beings through practical experiments. Along with the visible beings, there obviously also exist the invisible beings, the "devas" for example, who seek and support the cooperation with human beings on another level of consciousness. We have recognized that there is no limit to the community of life, neither above nor below. Above, high spiritual beings operate on ascending levels. Below, microscopically small beings operate on descending levels. The "school of life" which is arising in Tamera has had the marvelous idea of integrating the bacteria of the biogas plant into their community concept. While at the moment this is still a bit humorous it could soon become a serious matter of course.

Chapter 26: Charter of Fundamental Rights for All Living Beings

At the heart of a charter for a planetary order of peace is the new alliance of the human being with all co-creatures, the right of all beings to live, and the sacredness of life. The following list gives more detail to the objective ethics listed in Chapter 21; it applies to all stations of the Terra Nova movement:

1. All beings – humans, animals, and plants – have their special meaning and their special function within the structure of creation. All have the right to thrive, free from fear, according to the truth of their nature. From this it follows that:

2. All beings have the right to free movement, which they require for their development, their joy, and their physical and mental health. They must not be shackled or caged.

3. The bodies of all beings have grown special parts for coming in contact with the world: limbs, genitals, wings, horns, talons, tails, fins and so on. They must not be mutilated for this hinders their engagement with the world.

4. All beings originate from a world of protection and trust. All have the right to develop in this trust throughout their entire lives. All have the right to the fundamental health and freedom resulting from trust.

5. All beings have the right to nutrition in natural and healthy life conditions.

6. All non-human beings are part of the great family of life, as are we. They are therefore our friends and partners in evolution.

Chapter 27: The Worldwide Network – Global Campus and Terra Nova School

The Global Campus is a worldwide educational platform for building models of self-sufficiency, which make it possible to step out of the system of violence. Sabine Lichtenfels, in cooperation with Benjamin von Mendelssohn, developed this idea of a world university during international pilgrimages between 2005 and 2010. Since then international camps take place in different crisis areas where the material, social, mental, and spiritual foundations of Terra Nova are conveyed. The base station of the Global Campus is located in the Tamera peace research center in Portugal. Those involved are projects and people who have decided to collaborate on a global level. They see the need for new peace models and are committed to realizing them. At the core of this work is also a new alliance of humans with all co-creatures, as well as the development of decentralized, self-sufficient systems. For peace to be achieved on the outside, it is crucial that it arises on the inside among human beings. The project orients itself, both in theory and practice, along the following guidelines:

❖ Realigning the human world within the universal order of life.
❖ Establishing functioning communities.
❖ Ending the war between the genders and all sexual humiliation.
❖ Truth in love; no betrayal in partnerships.
❖ No revenge; grace instead of retaliation.
❖ Adhering to the objective ethics.
❖ Non-violent cooperation with all co-creatures.
❖ Healing water through the development of "Water Retention Landscapes."
❖ Developing Permaculture and self-sufficient food supplies.
❖ Withdrawal from the oil industry and the development of autonomous energy systems.

These criteria apply to the collaboration of the projects within the Global Campus and serve as guidelines for universities and ways of living within the forthcoming world society. These will bring in a new planetary order for the coexistence of all beings according to the laws of the Sacred Matrix. In autumn 2013, the Global Campus held workshops in five different countries: Colombia, Brazil, Kenya, Israel-Palestine, and Portugal. Forty people from Tamera traveled to these places to encounter the reality in which our global partners live, to assist them in creating ecological and technological facilities, and to exchange knowledge of how communities function.

Another organ in the worldwide network is the Terra Nova School. It consists of groups that study the basic thoughts of this work and spread this new information. They celebrate Global Grace Day annually on November 9th to make the perspective of Terra Nova publicly visible around the world. All who understand and love the thoughts of Terra Nova are invited to support these groups or to initiate a new group themselves. May the network of this school's stations span around the globe in the new era, as did the network of banks and corporations in the old!

Chapter 28: The Secret of Water

Whoever knows the secret of water possesses the power.[1]

~ Viktor Schauberger

Global healing work requires healthy water. We need another way of managing water if humanity is to survive. All specialists know that we will enter into planetary catastrophe within a few years if the conventional ways of managing water continue. The first condition for survival consists in restoring the original water cycles. In a natural water cycle rainwater is absorbed into the ground and resurfaces through springs. Thus purified – it is the best quality drinking water – it makes its way into streams, creeks, and rivers, all the way to the sea. However when forests are felled, aquifers drained, and water dammed in oversized reservoirs, the original cycles become distorted. Water becomes ever scarcer and soon potable water is no longer available.

"Water decreases" – this is a special topic on which Viktor Schauberger's research focused. He asserted that the amount of water on Earth is not constant and that the behavior of mankind is a determining factor. Water arises naturally in many places if it is not obstructed by human activity. Schauberger also claimed that water can be "produced" in any quantity, anywhere on Earth. We thereby encounter a theme of water research, so new and overwhelming that a separate book should be dedicated to it. Not surprisingly, Schauberger's advanced water concept caught the attention of those in political power – of course Hitler's engineers and later the Americans realized how explosive an issue water is. As a result, Schauberger was kidnapped several times to work in secret government units.

About the cultural meaning of water Schauberger writes,

Everything originated from water. Therefore water is the universal resource of every culture or the foundation of every physical, mental, and spiritual development. Unveiling the secret of water will put an end to all manner of speculation with its excesses, to which belong war, hatred, envy, intolerance and discord of every kind. The exhaustive investigation of water therefore truly signifies the end of all monopolies, the end of all domination and the beginning of a socialism arising from the development of individualism in its most perfect form.[2]

Water is a carrier of global information. The anthroposophist flow researcher Theodor Schwenk[3] says that the outer surfaces of many small currents that arise in whirling and flowing water, contain the information of the world. If we augment such findings with the research of those such as Viktor Schauberger, Masaru Emoto[4], and Sepp Holzer[5] we gain a completely new understanding of the being of water and about the meaning of water for life on Earth. Water distributes the information of life all over the globe, including the new information of Terra Nova. We have entered the Age of Aquarius but one need not believe in astrology in order to sense that we are approaching a future in which water will play a fundamental role.

Chapter 29: Religion – The Existence of the Divine World

Three million people gathered when Pope Francis arrived in Rio de Janeiro in 2013. That evening, many did not want to leave and so took their sleeping bags to Copacabana Beach where they spent the night. Two million young people slept on the beach to stay within the spirit of his message. The aerial photography shows a line of sleeping bags stretching all the way to the horizon. I ask readers to take a moment to reflect on what happened here. Behind the worldwide unrest lies the longing of young people for deeper answers to their life questions. What would happen if a global peace movement actually had an answer to humanity's religious question? The question of religion is certainly not a private matter; it is a global one.

We come from a higher world, of which we (as yet) know very little. Therein lies the anchor and mystery of all life, all growth and all love. In order to orient ourselves with greater certainty, to take meaningful actions and make realistic plans, we need to connect with this meta-world. We need to get to know the logic of its workings, its laws and how things connect within it. Schauberger said that power is held by those who know the secret of water.[1] We could claim likewise that those who know the religious secret of love have the "power." This is a gentle power which defines the new era. The religious secret of love is at the root of all things.

This is precisely why state and church have done everything possible to keep people from real divine sources – those who are connected with these sources are not easily governable. The subjugation of people to the status of minion required depriving them of their sexual and religious sources. Jesus' message was falsified and suppressed by the Catholic priesthood in the same way the cult of Isis was by the old (male) priesthood of Egypt. We are coming from an epoch marked by battle against the divine world. Whoever came too close to God, like Master Eckhart for example, were eliminated. (Master Eckhart died early enough; otherwise he would have been burnt as heretic.)

The human being is a manifestation of God, whoever or whatever this might be. We are the manifestation of a universe we carry within. The physiological universe of our cells and ganglia is coupled with the soul's universe of our thoughts, dreams, memories, ambitions, and abilities. The society of the future will be based on new knowledge of humankind and its inner connection to the cosmic entity which we refer to as God. We are only at the beginning – in the embryonic stages of our own development.

Due to a malign historic development, the human being was dislodged from his sources. Today we are confronted with the reality that there is hardly anyone still authentically connected with his or her religious wellspring. The human being of our time no longer aligned with the great power circuit of life and therefore uses substitute circuits that drive him increasingly off track. Both the religious and the sexual power circuits need to been newly installed so our future plans come back into the flow of the higher reality. Human society needs a new operating system.

We live in a "multiverse" in which there are many parallel worlds. The Brazilian medium Francisco Xavier claims that on some days more non-incarnated than incarnated people walk the streets of Rio de Janeiro.[2] I receive this kind of information with a mixture of humor and curiosity. What really happens after death? Which families, communities, networks, colonies, and cities exist in the beyond? When we dream at night, where is it that our spirit travels to? Our world is going through a fierce transformation and it could be that a tremendous door will soon open to the inquiring mind. As I see it, our situation is captured in this wonderful piece by Útmutató a Léleknek…

In a mother's womb were two babies.
One asked the other: "Do you believe in life after delivery?"
The other replied, "Why, of course. There has to be something after delivery. Maybe we are here to prepare ourselves for what we will be later."
"Nonsense," said the first. "There is no life after delivery. What kind of life would that be?"
The second said, "I don't know, but there will be more light than here. Maybe we will walk with our legs and eat from our mouths. Maybe we will have other senses that we can't understand now."
The first replied, "That is absurd. Walking is impossible. And eating with our mouths? Ridiculous! The umbilical cord supplies nutrition and everything we need. But the umbilical cord is so short. Life after delivery is to be logically excluded."

The second insisted, "Well I think there is something and maybe it's different than it is here. Maybe we won't need this physical cord anymore."

The first replied, "Nonsense. And moreover if there is life, then why has no one has ever come back from there? Delivery is the end of life, and in the after-delivery there is nothing but darkness and silence and oblivion. It takes us nowhere."

"Well, I don't know," said the second, "but certainly we will meet Mother and she will take care of us."

The first replied "Mother? You actually believe in Mother? That's laughable. If Mother exists then where is She now?"

The second said, "She is all around us. We are surrounded by her. We are of Her. It is in Her that we live. Without Her this world would not and could not exist."

Said the first: "Well I don't see Her, so it is only logical that She doesn't exist."

To which the second replied, "Sometimes, when you're in silence and you focus and you really listen, you can perceive Her presence, and you can hear Her loving voice, calling down from above."[3]

When we begin to think about the whole in which we live day to day, it is strangely disconcerting. We believe in the existence of something "out there," but we have lost the "mother." Authentic religious connection allows the disconcertment in the human soul to be replaced by an innermost knowing of trust, love, and home. This longing for home, consciously or unconsciously, runs through all of humanity. Religion is way by which this longing can be fulfilled.

Religion relates to our connectedness with the divine world. This world, which is not far from us, not above us, surrounds and permeates us with every breath we take. We were created by this world and in it we breathe, think, and love. We are made of its matter and the more we develop the more similar we, the embryonic human beings, become to our "creator" – until we ourselves are one with the divine world of which we were as ignorant as the twins in their mother's belly. What a profound parable! Hardly any system change could be more radical than that within religion. The use of the word "religion" in a revolutionary context is easily misunderstood. The new religion has no church, no orthodoxy, and no confession; it is a state of consciousness. It is a very vital state which leads to a new mode of function for our physical organs, heals "incurable" diseases, and performs great miracles. Every person will have his or her own experience. **The new concept of religion is not concerned with rising up after death, but of resurrecting before death – in this very life. The religion of the resurrected human being no longer means submitting to an overpowering God, but on the contrary, elevation to the divine reality from which we originate and to which we forever belong.** The new religiousness is physical and sensual. It opens our channels to the sources of love, healing, and art. It opens our channels to children. It opens gates for scientific thinking of which we could previously only dream. Religion is the filling of our souls with belief that "can move mountains." I mean this almost literally. "We" can reshape the world in accordance with the Sacred Matrix to the degree that we find this form of belief. I put "we" in quotes, for it is no longer we ourselves that bring about the shift, but the POWER operating through us. In this state, we experience what it means to be happy. As Prentice Mulford writes, "*it is the greatest happiness of man to be a channel for the spiritual powers of the universe.*"[4]

It will take a while for the new religion to gain acceptance in the coming culture. It is an historical process comparable to that of free sexuality. It will come into being everywhere, for the existence of the divine world is a reality we can no longer ignore. It is not a question of belief or disbelief, but of seeing and knowing. The degree to which it will become effective in our lives depends on our inner opening and readiness. Religion cannot be understood when the heart is closed. It is not ideological to acknowledge the divine world; it is ideological to deny it. The fight still currently waged against religion by journalism and science is based in ignorance that will soon cease to exist.

How do we transform disbelief to belief? How does the unborn child answer when asked if it believes in the existence of the mother? How would a fish answer if asked whether it believes in the existence of water? We live in the divine world in the way that fish live in water. How can we believe or not believe in something that is always there and which permanently surrounds us? Master Eckhart's clarity on this is that, "*God is always with us, we however are not always at home.*"[5] Why are we not always at home? **It is often the case that we are so intensely captured by secret love issues that we are no longer receptive to information from the divine world, even if we are trying. When we are under the spell of an unresolved love issue, our soul is occupied.** The whole world is unconsciously occupied by a collective trauma in love. This is why the master plan of the Healing Biotopes intends to link its "seminary" with the Love School. It will

174

require diligence for us to dissolve the historic trauma so that we once again become receptive to the information and power from the higher world.

The loss of belief in the divine world is an historic phenomenon and cannot be attributed to our individual narrow-mindedness. Nevertheless it is up to us to step out of this historic narrow-mindedness and to come to accept the facts. As humans we are part of a divine world and it would be natural to believe that. The divinity of our nature is as obvious as our physical existence. No one would doubt their divine nature if the original trust had not been destroyed through the ravages of history. It is our historic and global task to find religious belief self-evident again. Life is compassion; life is trust; life is love; life is religion.

When we believe in our divine nature the qualities inherent to that nature are revealed to us: faculties of thinking, of love, and healing. As K.O. Schmidt has so beautifully written...

> We recognize that we live as spirit-beings in a spiritual universe and share in its powers and possibilities as soon and as far as we faithfully affirm it... And only because we, as fainthearted ones, have all thus far had too little confidence in ourselves, did we not yet dare to assert and act on our true greatness as children of God and carriers of all divine powers. We have to date only activated a minute fraction of the powers waiting in us for their engagement through us.

> It is strange that is it so hard for us to understand this most simple of all truths and that we are so tentative in taking the positive consequences of belief and trust in the reality of our harmony and communion with the infinite, and to live in consciousness of reality, that is to live free of worry, healthily and happily from the spirit.[6]

This background offers us another perspective on reality. From this we can recognize anew the particular gift bequeathed to us in the area of healing. When a cancerous tumor shrinks to nothing within seconds or when compressed tissue returns to its healthy state in a very short time, it does not mean that natural laws are broken or abolished, but that they are extended and complemented by higher powers.

As we become inwardly compatible with the Sacred Matrix, we can receive the powers of the divine world. This natural law carries an ethical obligation, for we need to abide by the rules of the divine world in order to reach compatibility with it. With the firm decision to follow these rules – the guidelines of the objective ethics – we gain access to the higher potency that we need for the work of global transformation. A community that operates in the field of higher powers is spared a great deal of work for they live, without irony, according to the maxim, *"let go and let God."*

Religion is no school subject and no ecclesiastic confession, but a state of being. We all originate from the divine milieu, live in it, and remain in it after death, for the divine milieu is the world, the universe. The secret of God is the secret of the universe; it shines toward us in every blossoming flower. When we consciously return to our primordial religious state of being, we experience this not as ecstasy, but calmly as a matter of fact. We are simply at the place we are meant to be. It is about time that we become visible to each other in this way and that we establish places for the divine world to find home here on Earth. This is precisely what we are doing with the Healing Biotopes project. We are continuing something that was initiated many hundreds of years ago by Buddha, Ashoka, Jesus, Mani, and founders of other religions. However we are lifting it to a new level by integrating the feminine source and by developing a new social order to enable its realization. Religious instructions have to date been directed toward the individual. Now, we are developing collective systems for "enlightenment," which means we develop **social structures which enable the connection with the divine world for all**. The idea is fundamentally about bringing the "kingdom of God" down to Earth – into our ways of living and our places of work; into the realms of our thoughts and love relationships. Eros and religion are the two fundamental forces of life which today, after a violent history of separation and suppression, rise in union and lead us to the primordial ground where they meet and become one.

Is this conceivable? People have tried a thousand ways to reach God. They have fasted and flagellated themselves; humbled and elevated themselves; lived as hermits in the desert and built cathedrals. They have done everything possible but for one thing: they have not accepted the gift of erotic love and so have not corrected the mistaken taboos under which they suffered so harshly. They have excluded and fought against Eros. Male-dominated religion pitched itself against Eros, which is why it has caused such terrible disasters. **Eros and religion belong together! Religion without Eros becomes cold, rigid and cruel. Without God Eros cannot be fulfilling in the long run because it loses itself in excess, jealousy, and violence. There is a lot** of focus today on "sustainability;" we wish for a sustainable erotic joy that lasts through our lifetime and continues through our descendants. The reunification of Eros and religion is the basis for a new civilization on our planet.

Chapter 30: Political Theory

Field Powers and the Morphogenetic World Process: The Expansion and Growth of Terra Nova

Earth and all life in her biosphere form a Holon, an open system with the characteristics of a living organism. If we enter new energy or information at any one point it affects the entire organism. Acupuncture and many medical applications are based on this principle. Within the planet's bio-system the entering of new information initiates that which we call the "morphogenetic world process." This is the core of the global healing concept that we in Tamera refer to as the "Political Theory." Due to the fundamental importance of this concept we want to shed more light on it.

Life is a web in which everything from microorganisms to human beings is interlinked in diverse ways: the neurons in the human brain, the organs in our bodies, the living beings in the biosphere, and the bodies of water on Earth. The intercommunication of the molecules in a cell all the way to the intercommunication of the galaxies in the cosmos constitutes a multi-dimensional system of the highest complexity; a kind of cosmic Internet, which generates and conveys life's information. There are sensors and receptors absorbing and relaying this information everywhere. The network of life is a network of information.

When we enter new information into the network it will take effect everywhere provided an appropriate receptor (the human brain for example) is in place. When information and thoughts occur that are of great importance to the whole it becomes highly probable that they will soon be thought everywhere. I assume this will even be the case for thoughts that today might seem far-fetched or unrealistic, such as the ideas of free sexuality, cooperation with wild animals, communication with natural spirits, and that all diseases can be healed. In our project we have learned that new thoughts, so long as they are consistent with evolutionary logic, prevail quickly and easily when the way is not blocked by prejudice. *"Nothing is stronger than an idea whose time has come."*[1]

All of evolution works through the **law of fields**. Whenever a new discovery is made, one of importance for the development of a species, a new "morphogenetic field" arises that makes new information operative in all members of that population. Throughout the evolution of life there have been many such cases of renewal. The development from the single-cell organism to the human being would not otherwise have been possible. From the emergence of the first cell – resulting from a particular combination of amino acids and other organic molecules – an almighty morphogenetic field was generated which resulted in the oceans teeming with single-cell beings. The development of the nucleus followed, the formation of a biological core, again giving rise to a new field. Every stage since has activated the morphogenetic field process, which step by step, led to the genesis of the human being.

Human civilization also unfolds according to field law. This can be seen in our social, technological and scientific achievements and our physical abilities. The emergence of monotheistic religion, the invention of the steam engine, the use of fossil fuels, the ascent of Mount Everest without oxygen support, and the abstract art movement are further examples of field formation. **Whenever an innovation is made which is interesting or important to a certain population, that discovery no longer needs to be worked out by successive individuals for it is already palpable as a latent possibility and can be recalled as needed.** A beautiful example of this is the spreading of graffiti art around the world. Hardly had the walls of the metropolises been filled with this sophisticated art, when it could already be discovered on the ruins of remote farmhouses in the Portuguese Alentejo.

Once the first Healing Biotopes – Water Retention Landscapes with Permaculture and functioning community – really thrive they will appear everywhere, so long as they are not blocked by military violence. As we build them a spiritual field will condense on Earth. The noosphere takes on an "excited state," which will greatly increase the probability of further Healing Biotopes arising. The information of the new culture will be received everywhere that human consciousness is ready for it. Missionary work is not necessary but we do need to develop the information to the point at which it is mature enough to generate a new field. The endurance of internal contradictions is an indication that the information has not yet reached the morphogenetic maturity necessary for its dissemination.

Whenever people live in the frequency of life, and are therefore of clear mind, the new information can be retrieved. The ethics of free sexuality, the symbiosis of free sexuality and partnership, the precepts of the objective ethics, a fundamentally compassionate disposition and the implications of a sacred alliance with all fellow beings will occur in the imaginations of people worldwide. These are expressions of the objective universal figure of Terra Nova. As soon as it is manifested in one place, it can manifest everywhere.

The women from Turkey, Bolivia, and Togo that attended Tamera's Summer University in 2013 now need a lot of support to manifest this new information at home. They are actors in a world process that is carried by the truth of universal life. We felt that love connected us with these women. It was a sense of the universal love that hits us when we see the image of Terra Nova sensually embodied. This image signifies the solidarity and cooperation among all peoples in the creation of a worldwide holy land. We have to connect it with a new image for the love between the genders wherein free love and partner love find themselves harmoniously intertwined. As soon as this image is freed from contradiction it will trigger the formation of a morphogenetic field, for it corresponds with the laws of the Sacred Matrix. As soon as the first Healing Biotopes really function in the sense of a deeper coherence with the laws of love, they will prevail worldwide, because love is something that everyone likes.

Where morphogenetic fields are set in motion, special "field powers" begin to operate. We can observe a small example of the effect of field powers in fire-walking. Somewhere someone proved that one could walk barefoot over glowing coals. This gave rise to a worldwide fire-walking "movement" in which participants could cross a seven meter-long carpet of burning coals without hurting themselves. This was made possible by the power of fields, without which most participants would certainly have burned their feet. The field power is generated through information. In this case the information that "it is possible." The case of Reinhold Messner's ascent of Everest without additional oxygen is similar in that his achievement also released the new information that "this is possible" and many people could then follow suit.

The kind of "leap" that applied to fire walking can also be made in social and sexual arenas. As soon as an idea spreads, the inner switch can turn from "impossible" to "possible," from "no" to "yes," from "ugly" to "wonderful." The variability of human judgment is nearly limitless. It is not questions of individual taste, but field powers that will integrate free sexuality into the planetary community. The same holds true for nonviolent behavior toward animals, for abolishing slaughterhouses, for discovering the Sacred Matrix, for implementing the global Healing Biotopes plan, and eventually for the entire global revolution. The revolution will end the world process of capitalism and replace it with a highly interconnected system of decentralized, autonomous communities. That which is currently working only crudely in some groups will tomorrow be the cultural treasure of all humanity. Social and sexual renewal will assume a central position in the new culture – as will the principles of decentralized water, food, and energy supplies. Independent, free communities will follow principles of regional subsistence economy on their land and share their surplus with those in their surroundings. There will no longer be foreign powers watching over their land and demanding money for its use. The curse of the past will have ended. How could we have gone so far astray? **We will lift this spell by establishing a powerful morphogenetic field of liberation.**

More than seven billion people need to organize themselves anew. A collective shift of this scale is possible within the power of a field. The power of fields is generated by the centers and projects, the movements and events that people all over the world undertake for the creation of Terra Nova. The great transformation that we are currently going through is a profound shift from one field of power to another. Within the new field we no longer submit to an overpowering God, but activate the God we carry within us. We do not increase our strength by dominating nature, but by cooperating with it. New intellectual and spiritual power fields are arising for the fundamental issues of life, from the material basis to the soul realms of Eros and religion. According to the principle of spiritual attraction, every power field draws the potential for manifestation towards itself. Those who activate within themselves the power field of love attract all that serves love. When we establish the power field of a Healing Biotope it will attract all that serves its realization. The work we need to do consists above all in establishing new power fields of intellect and spirit. It will serve every new Healing Biotope to have a school and a "church" to establish and affirm the new intellectual and spiritual power fields. In Tamera we hold a "matinee" every Sunday, a gathering in which the intellectual and spiritual foundations of our work are revisited and affirmed.

Outside there is a big sunflower. It is nine in the morning; its bloom faces the east. At noon it will salute the south as it follows the path of the sun. Its movement happens "by itself"; no effort is needed. This heavy flower finds itself in the power field of the sun and therefore requires no individual mechanical power to carry out its movement. **It is worthwhile to pause here, to reflect a moment on the miracle of invisible power fields and their effect on the material world.** Nearly everything seems possible for the human being when he is able to activate the appropriate power field. A man ties himself between two cars that then drive in opposite directions; they cannot move from the spot because the man has activated a power field wherein he cannot be ripped apart. This actually happened.

Religion, Eros, love, community, home, trust, solidarity, and cooperation are fundamental to human existence. If a new power field is created for these, we will have accumulated the power of the morphogenetic world process that will bring about a new civilization. If the worldwide power field for Terra Nova is established successfully we will experience the jubilation of a world that had suffered too long under the nefarious tyranny of the old fields of power.

PART V
TAMERA: A GLOBAL PEACE SCHOOL

Chapter 31: The Tamera Project

So long as there is a single child starving, one single animal tortured, one African girl circumcised, one woman raped, one person mistreated on the grounds of their faith, one young person forced to go to war then our world is in disorder. It is our definitive task to free this world from such atrocious pain. We could always say "this is an illusion," but as soon as our eyes start to open, as soon as we see the suffering of these victims, as soon as we ourselves are one of these tortured beings, there is just a single cry – the cry for relief.[1]

This extract is taken from one of our foundational texts. It is because we have heard this cry that we have done everything in our power to find an answer. The extent of global violence required approaches to peace work that far exceeded conventional concepts. In May 1978, a project was founded in Germany under the name "Bauhuette" [Builder's Lodge], from which the project "Tamera" in Portugal originated.

It has been from the beginning an interdisciplinary research project which drew intimate connections between the fields of nature, community, and spirituality. Issues of sexuality have been as important as questions of ethics and theology. Our work has been about shaping the material, social, intellectual, and spiritual conditions of our cohabitation with the aim of creating on the one hand, a functioning community and on the other a generalizable perspective of global peace work. At the center of our work was and is a new bond between masculine and feminine powers, a new love between the genders, a new cooperation with the beings of nature, and a new connection with the powers and laws of the divine world. Our objective is to establish "Biosphere III" – a comprehensive model of regional self-sufficiency linked to a university where the basic issues of Terra Nova are researched and taught, while internal education takes place in the "Political Ashram."

While the social atmosphere has often been turbulent, ours has always remained a research and peace project. As founders, we needed time and again to correct our assumptions and ways behaving. The clash with contemporary ways of thinking was severe; it was difficult to come safely through the aforementioned vilification and harassment.

It seems that this too was part of our curriculum. The work of all community members was and is aimed at activating thoughts of peace and healing in all conflicts. This also applies to internal love relationships. Seeing where the project has arrived today, I am sure that the work done so far has laid essential ground for a coming peace culture. The ethical, social, and ecological information developed is fertile soil for the germination of the new global society. The project orients itself in both theory and practice along the guideline of a new global culture in harmony with life, the Earth, and all fellow beings, as has been described in this book. At the core lies the development of a new humaneness based on trust and compassion and the creation of a model of life wherein this humaneness can endure.

Approximately one hundred and sixty people live and work in Tamera. There is a children's center, the "Escola da Esperança" (a combined primary and secondary school) a center for adult learning, and a school for feminine peace knowledge. Parallel to this is an ecology center, a technology department, a department for regional autonomy, an experimental hectare for the cooperation with visible and invisible beings, a self-sufficient Solar Village test field, a Love School and an office for international networking and information exchange (the Institute for Global Peace Work). All of this has arisen, from scratch, over the course of twenty years on an area of 330 acres.

In her book about Tamera, the journalist Leila Dregger writes,

A walk through Tamera today takes one through cascades of lakes and ponds, on the shores of which grow the permaculture gardens used for both teaching and food supply. In the coming years the water landscape will be expanded and completed, so that the trees on the hills will also be able to grow again and return to health.

The summer kitchen of the Solar Village test field demonstrates techniques for cooking with solar energy and biogas, electricity generation, food preservation, and pumping water. Almost all of the systems were built in Tamera's own workshops. In the research greenhouse new technologies are tested which are intended to free settlements of the future from dependence on centralized energy supply systems.

On the building sites, simple traditional construction techniques are combined with modern architectural

188

concepts. Participants of the peace education programs study in seminar rooms and the auditorium. Theatre and music groups rehearse for their performances on the stages of the Aula. The participants of the Youth School for Global Learning are being taught by young adults who were students themselves here a few years ago.

Men and women from different countries and cultures are working together to support the development of the new systems. They contribute their knowledge and experience and gain insights, which they will use for the creation of autonomous settlements in their home countries...

The most important aspect in all of this is coming together. People who previously learned to perceive each other as enemies, for example those from Israel and Palestine, are working here hand-in-hand. Common work toward a higher goal, more important for the people of both "sides" than the conflict, leaves no space for hostility. Responsibility for the whole and mutual support are the basic ethical guidelines for living together in Tamera...

Through this combination a worldwide network of different groups and initiatives has developed, all connected with Tamera to bring its knowledge to their projects, or to create new projects based on similar principles. Young people love to invest all their energy and joy into such a planetary perspective.

Let us now take a look at the world. We direct our attention not towards today's metropolitan areas, but to the places where new centers for peace are developing. If we look closely, we discover the signs of a global renaissance. Gentle yet unstoppable, a powerful movement is forming, a movement for reconnection with nature and reconciliation with each other in the certainty of a different future – a movement for a free Earth.[2]

The development of Tamera has now reached a point where we are able to offer a cogent concept for self-sufficiency to those areas of our planet in the direst crises, and a firm material basis for their

189

autonomy. We are thinking of regions like Haiti after the 2010 earthquake or the Philippines after the 2013 typhoon. Empowered by the morphogenetic field of the new culture, devastated areas could be rebuilt and given new orientation. Instead of sinking hopelessly into poverty they could turn into birth-places for a new era of civilization. It is very simple – those who came out last in global competition could move to the forefront of the planetary development. If international aid organizations succeed in manifesting the new ecological and social ideas in these kinds of crisis areas these places will be connected to the power field of Terra Nova. They will therefore, after centuries of enslavement and exploitation, be at the beginning of an evolution headed toward autonomy, freedom, and membership in the new planetary community. In order to take this research to its necessary maturity, we need the support of experts as well as financial support to sponsor people from crisis regions, who are eager to learn, to come to Tamera to study the principles and examples of decentralized autonomy models, and to implement them in their countries.

Over the course of thirty-seven years a network of socially and politically engaged people formed, which will not fail due to human conflict. It was an absolutely inconceivable, incredible journey that no one could possibly have foreseen. Many have left the project; new people have joined. It will be a lasting memory for all who have participated. I thank all who have gone with us through thick and thin. Some have children who are now as old as they themselves were when they entered; four generations live together here. I thank the community for the solidarity and cohesion it has shown through the difficult times and I thank our spiritual guidance without which we would barely have survived some of our most severe challenges. Our work continues. Ahead of us lies the creation of "Biosphere III," as well as building a "Universal Hall," a gathering place for global peace workers. The continuation of our work will rely on expert knowledge and financial assistance. The morphogenetic world process is still in its early stages. We invite new activists, the Terra Nova School groups, and all friends in the network to help make this work a success.

On behalf of all lovers.
On behalf of all children.
On behalf of all creatures.
Thank you and Amen!

Tamera in Pictures

Sabine Lichtenfels,
co-founder of Tamera,
head of the Global Love
School

Dieter Duhm,
co-founder of Tamera,
initiator of the Healing
Biotopes Plan

In Tamera's auditorium

Building a biogas plant with Thomas H. Culhane (left)
in Tamera

Tamera's Solar Village test-field

Vasamalli Kurtaz, representative of the Todas tribe in
India, cooks with some children from Tamera

Children's Theater, *"The Black Shadow and the Riddle
of the Princess."*

Before the construction of the Water Retention
Landscape in Tamera

Building a Water Retention space

Retention Landscape after creating "Lake 1"

Tamera's recovering nature

Grace Pilgrimage in Israel-Palestine

Grace Pilgrimage in Colombia

Stone Circle in Évora, Portugal

Tibetan lamas offer a blessing to Sabine Lichtenfels
in Tamera

SD Forum during an art course

Inner and outer movements in the SD Forum

Exercises of courage in a study group

Art Course

We love pigs

Olive Harvest in Tamera

After the harvest

(Left) Global Campus in a Sao Paulo, Brazil favela (slum)
(Right) Praying with the Global Campus in Tamera

Encounter with the military, Global Campus, Colombia

Glossary

Agathon: Greek for "the good," the highest or supreme good in a moral sense, *summum bonum*. According to Plato, it cannot be precisely explained; but once it is seen, it allows one to understand all else.[1]

Akashic Records: Term coined by theosophy and anthroposophy in the late 1800s from *akasha*, the Sanskrit word for "sky," "space," "luminous," or "æther," referring to an all-encompassing world memory in immaterial form.[2]

Alpha Frequency: Also referred to as "alpha waves." Neural oscillations in the frequency range of 7.5–12.5 Hz arising from coherent electrical activity in the human brain, associated with states of higher consciousness and healing effects for the organism. The alpha frequency is apparently compatible with the Schumann resonance of the Earth's electromagnetic field.

Ananda: Pali and Sanskrit word for "bliss." Referred to as the state of primordial joy of life in Indian philosophy.

Assemblage point: Term coined by Carlos Castañeda. The epicenter of energy within the human energy field, "the point where perception is assembled." It is considered central to both our psychological and physical existence. In *The Power of Silence*, Castañeda writes, "When the assemblage point shifts, it makes possible the perception of an entirely different world – as objective and factual as the one we normally perceive."[3]

Body Armor: Term coined by Wilhelm Reich.[4] According to his research, healthy organisms and organs have natural expansion and contraction; it is the pulsation of life energy. When human organisms are "armored," their pulsation is disturbed and movement restricted. This is experienced as a lack of aliveness, constant tension and often leads to disease and violence.

Carrier Wave: An electromagnetic wave that can be modulated in frequency, amplitude, or phase to transmit information. In this book the term is used in a rather figurative sense for the fundamental underlying vibration of Terra Nova, able to convey the specific features of that new field all over the world.

Christ Code: The informational matrix of the Christ Nature within the human soul and genetic code.

Christ Impulse: The cultural impulse for manifesting the Christ Nature in human coexistence and society, which has historically been carried by many individuals and movements in various cultures and religions.

Christ Nature: Term coined by Wilhelm Reich. What he calls the original human essentiality, which is intrinsically creative, compassionate and capable of loving; free of fear, greed and narcissism, as well as of intentions for control and domination. According to Reich, every newborn child is a potential "new Christ."[5] In similar ways, Rudolf Steiner describes the cosmic entity embodying these qualities as Christ consciousness.

Collective Trauma: Term coined by Dieter Duhm. Describes the transpersonal and deeply rooted structure of fear that more or less all modern people carry within themselves, as a result of several millennia of war, suppression, and genocide. (See Chapter 3)

Concrete Utopia: Term coined by Ernst Bloch. The state after a possible change of society. It is "utopia becoming concrete."[6] (See Chapter 13)

Deva: Sanskrit word for deity; spiritual entities behind animals and all beings of nature; also referred to as the group soul of a species.[7]

Emotional Body: The ethereal layer of the human organism associated with feelings, emotions, and the interpretations of events. As the emotional and physical layers of the body are interconnected, the emotional body influences physical processes.

Entelechy: Originally developed by Aristotle in his teachings of potentiality and actuality, can be translated as "being at an end."[8] It is the highest goal and potential of perfection inherent to every living being. According to the biologist Hans Driesch the entelechy is the "non-physical causal factor" that organizes morphogenesis and underlies the genetic code. The entelechy is present at any stage of development, however small or imperfect or alienated a being may be. It is the natural intention of and within living beings driving their growth toward perfection.

Excited State: State in which an atom or molecule carries a higher energy than the basic energy level. Used metaphorically in this book for the situation when the potential for radical societal change builds due to increasing transformative energies.

Fields of Potentiality: Term coined by Werner Heisenberg. Describes quantum particles as fields of potentiality rather than as firm and definite matter. "Natural science does not simply describe and explain nature: it describes nature as exposed to our method of questioning."[9] Quantum particles exist in a superposition of latent states and it is due to the observer that they manifest at certain spots as material particles.

Free Love: Love free of fear and possessiveness. A culture of human coexistence that allows love to grow, wherein free sexuality and partnership are no longer contradictory, but complement one another.

Free Sexuality: An erotic culture based on trust, contact, and solidarity where the sexual relation between people does not depend on relationship or partnership commitments. Freedom in sexuality however is not a matter of the quantity of sexual partners or any other external form, but rather of following one's own truth and desire and of being part of a social order that allows one to express that truth. This is why trust is a key for genuinely free sexuality. (See Chapter 20)

Hara: Japanese for 'abdomen.' Used as a technical anatomic term as well as for the energetic center located at the navel. It is the body's center of balance. Learning to be centered in the Hara and guiding its energies has been one of the essential capacities in Eastern spiritual traditions and martial arts to unfold power.

Hologram: Photographic recording of a light field that can be reconstructed as a three-dimensional image. A vast amount of information can be stored within a single photographic plate and different images can be selectively reconstructed depending on the angle of an incoming light beam. An increasing number of scientists have come to the conclusion that the entire universe works according to holographic principles, allowing us to shift from reality A to reality B by changing our point of view.

Holographic fabric of the world: Vision of the universe based on the oneness of all that exists; the world seen as unified whole. The information, structures and laws of the universe are reflected in all its parts and can therefore not only be retrieved, but also influenced from any point in space and time. Reality does not exist in an ultimate objective form, but rather as a constantly moving process of creation depending on the perspective of the observer.[10]

Holon: Derivation from the Greek word for "whole." Something that is both a whole and a part. Holons are evolving, self-organizing, and largely independent systems that are both comprised of subordinate holons and part of higher-level holons. All levels of organization in the universe – from the smallest systems in subatomic space to the largest systems in intergalactic space – can be described as holons.

Implicate Order: Concept coined by David Bohm.[11] Explains aspects of the holographic nature of reality. The implicate order, also called the "enfolded" order, refers to totality of existence with all its potentialities; the explicate order, also called the "unfolded order" to those aspects we perceive as a matter of fact. Bohm describes reality as a constant interplay between implicate and explicate order and says that the explicate relates to the implicate order as the water drop to the total amount of water in an ocean.

Metanoia: Greek word for "repentance." Signifies profound spiritual transformation, the journey of changing one's mind, heart, self, or way of life.

Morphogenetic Field: Immaterial information field that influences and determines the form or pattern of things and that stores the collective habits of species. According to Rupert Sheldrake, it is due to morphogenetic fields that as soon as something new is done somewhere it becomes easier and easier for it to be repeated anywhere.[12] Evolution moves forward by creating new fields. In this book the term is used in logical extension of its original form, applying the field theory to the societal and political realms. (See Chapter 30)

Noosphere: Term coined by Pierre Teilhard de Chardin in his Cosmogenesis.[13] It is the global sphere of information and human thought surrounding the Earth on an immaterial level, the spirit body of mankind and the Earth.

Original Matrix: The underlying informational pattern or blueprint of an organism. The *original matrix* is the inherent healing program of the organism anchored in its genetic code. It is present even in the case of severe disease, distortion, or alienation; its activation can bring about healing even in the most hopeless situations.

Orgone/Orgonotic: Term coined by Wilhelm Reich.[14] The universal life power, the omnipresent creative substance of the universe that leads to the organization of all stages of life, permeating all processes of the living world – the same way in both waters and clouds as well as our human physiological and psychological processes. One might also call it "Chi" (Taoism), "Prana" (Hinduism), or "élan vital" (Henri Bergson), et cetera.

Prehistoric Utopia: Term coined by Sabine Lichtenfels. The primordial entelechy vision of a human civilization embedded within creation and the Sacred Matrix. Even though Sabine Lichtenfels describes the Prehistoric Utopia in reference to tribal peace cultures in Portugal and Malta that existed before patriarchy, it applies to all times and stages of human evolution, even if its external features might differ throughout the centuries.

Psi: Derived from the 23rd letter of the Greek alphabet (ψ). Term used by parapsychologists for the unexplained power behind phenomena of extrasensory perception and telekinesis.

Sacred Geometry: The geometry used in planning and constructing sacred buildings such as temples, churches, cathedrals, et cetera. Sacred geometry attempts to express and manifest sacred symbols, patterns, and energies through certain geometrical forms and proportions.

Sacred Matrix: Universal pattern organizing the structures, laws, and movements of life on all levels of existence.[15] (See Chapter 8)

SD Forum: Abbreviation for "Selbstdarstellung" (German word for self-expression). A social tool for creating transparency and trust in a community as well as for individuals to widen their consciousness in relation to what are usually automatized or suppressed layers of their personality; a necessary element for building community. (See "SD Forum" in Chapter 19)

Sociosphere: The sphere of human interaction and society.

Spirit Body: Spiritual layer of the human organism, steered by consciousness, mind, and spirit. As consciousness moves energies and energies move matter, the spirit body influences the emotional, psychological, and physical processes within the organism.

Supramental: "Beyond the normal mind." Used by Sri Aurobindo for the "divine consciousness" or the "super-mind" of the upcoming new civilization.[16]

Tat Tvam Asi: Sanskrit phrase. Can be translated as "Thou art that." Originally appeared in the Chandogya Upanishad in a conversation between Uddalaka Aruni and his son Svetaketu.[17] The self – in its primal, original state – is identical with the ultimate reality from which everything originates.

Unio Mystica: Mystical state of oneness of the individual with the divine, often experienced as a form of ecstasy.

Water Retention Landscape: Form of decentralized water management introduced to revitalize damaged landscapes, restore the natural hydrological cycles, and reverse desertification. Water Retention Landscapes are designed after natural principles, in a way that rainwater falling on the land can be absorbed and thereby restore the soil and recharge the aquifer.[18]

Zoon Politikon: Term coined by Aristotle.[19] The Greek phrase is mostly translated as "political animal" or "political being."

About the Author

Dieter Duhm was born in 1942 in Berlin, Germany.

He has a PhD in sociology, in addition to being an art historian, author, and psychoanalyst. He is the initiator of the "Healing Biotopes Plan," a global peace plan.

In 1967, he joined the Marxist left and became one of the leading characters in the German students' movement. Here, he made a connection between the thoughts behind the political revolution and the thoughts related to the liberation of the individual; ideas that brought him recognition through his book *Angst im Kapitalismus* [*Fear in Capitalism*] (1972). Around 1975 he began publically distancing himself from the leftist dogmatism and turned to a quest for a more thorough social alternative.

In 1978, he established the "Bauhütte" project and led a three-year social experiment with 40 participants in the Black Forest in Germany. Its central focus was to "found a community for our times" and it embraced all the questions of the origin, meaning, and aim of human existence on planet Earth. The outlines of a new possibility for existence arose with the concepts of "free love," "spiritual ecology," and "resonance technology."

In 1995, he founded the Tamera peace research center in Portugal together with the theologian Sabine Lichtenfels and others. Today Tamera has approximately 160 co-workers.

Dieter Duhm has dedicated his life to creating an effective forum for a global peace initiative that can be a match for the destructive forces of capitalistic globalization.

For more information: www.dieter-duhm.com

Participation and Further Information

If you love the ideas expressed in this book and wish to deepen these perspectives, you are invited to join the Terra Nova School. It is dedicated to the study and manifestation of the social, spiritual and ecological foundations of a new global culture. Find out more at http://terra-nova-school.org

In order to manifest the vision of Terra Nova, this information needs to be seen and shared by more and more people around the world. Please help us to distribute it. We welcome every new activist and student for Terra Nova with joyful anticipation of our upcoming cooperation!

More information and contact:

Institute for Global Peace Work c/o Tamera
Monte do Cerro • P 7630-303 Colos, Portugal
Ph.: +351 - 283 635 484 • Fax: +351 - 283 635 374
E-Mail: igp@tamera.org • www.tamera.org

Financial Support

The Global Healing Biotopes plan relies on external financial support. The Grace Foundation raises and distributes money for the plan's implementation. For further information please visit: http://www.the-grace-foundation.org
We thank all donors for their generosity.

For donations in US Dollars:

Union Bank, 12885 Bonness Rd, Sonoma, CA 95476
Account holder: Inquiring Systems, Inc. / Grace Foundation
Acct. No.: 7960004390
Routing No.: 122000496

The Grace Foundation – America has 501c-3 status thanks to fiscal sponsorship provided by Inquiring Systems, Inc. Tax-deductible receipts can be issued.

For donations in Euros:

Raiffeisenbank Zürich
Account holder: Grace - Stiftung zur Humanisierung des
Geldes, Zürich
Acct. No.: 92188.69
IBAN: CH9881487000009218869
BIC: RAIFCH22
Clearing 81487

Tax-deductible receipts can be issued by Grace – Stiftung zur
Humanisierung des Geldes. The validity of these receipts outside of
Switzerland will vary according to local regulations.
If you require a receipt please write to The Grace Foundation at:
contact@the-grace-foundation.org

Works Cited

A list of references noted in the text, by chapter…

Foreword by the Author

1. Etty Hillesum, *An Interrupted Life: The Diaries and Letters of Etty Hillesum 1941–1943*, trans. Arnold J. Pomerans. (New York: Pantheon Books, 1984).

Introduction

1. Leila Dregger, "Gentle Power: Thoughts on a New Women's Movement," *Terra Nova Voice,* March 6, 2015, http://terranovavoice.tamera.org/2015/03/gentle-power-2/1509

Chapter 1: The Global Catastrophe

1. "Girl Rising: Malala Fires Up a New Generation," *Der Spiegel*, Issue 28/2013 (July 8, 2013).

Chapter 2: Revolution for Life

1. Sabine Lichtenfels, *Grace: Pilgrimage for a Future without War* (Wiesenburg: Verlag Meiga, 2007), 207.
2. *Ibid.*
3. Prentice Mulford, *Unfug Des Lebens Und Des Sterbens* (Frankfurt Am Main: Fischer Taschenbuch Verlag GmbH, 1977).
4. Logos Filmes, "Policial Lanasa Sua Arma No Fogo Em Protesto No Rio," *YouTube* (June 18, 2013), last accessed July 19, 2015, https://www.youtube.com/watch?feature=player_embedded&v=6FCllI qaXig.

Chapter 3: Collective Trauma – The Morphogenetic Field of Fear

1. Eva T. H. Brann, *The Logos of Heraclitus* (Philadelphia: Paul Dry Books, 2011).
2. Satprem and F. De Towarnicki, *My Burning Heart* (New York, NY: Institute for Evolutionary Research, 1989).

213

3. Claude Anshin Thomas, *At Hell's Gate: A Soldier's Journey from War to Peace* (Boston: Shambhala, 2005).
4. Eckhart Tolle, *A New Earth: Awakening to Your Life's Purpose* (New York: Plume, 2006).

Chapter 4: Destroyed Love

1. Craig S. Barnes, *In Search of the Lost Feminine: Decoding the Myths That Radically Reshaped Civilization* (Golden, CO: Fulcrum, 2006).
2. Saul Padover, "Introduction: Marx, the Human Side," *The Karl Marx Library Vol. VI: On Education, Women, and Children*. trans. and ed. Saul Padover (New York: McGraw Hill Book Co., 1975).
3. Dieter Duhm, *Angst Im Kapitalismus* (Lampertheim: Kübler, 1975).

Chapter 5: The Birth of a New Era

1. Pope Francis, "Evangelii Gaudium: Apostolic Exhortation on the Proclamation of the Gospel in Today's World (24 November 2013)," vatican.va, Point 59, last accessed July 19, 2015, http://w2.vatican.va/content/francesco/en/apost_exhortations/document s/papa-francesco_esortazione-ap_20131124_evangelii-gaudium.html.
2. *Id.*, Point 53.
3. Naomi Klein, *This Changes Everything: Capitalism vs. the Climate* (New York: Simon & Schuster, 2014).
4. Pierre Teilhard De Chardin, Julian Huxley, and Bernard Wall, *The Phenomenon of Man* (New York: Harper, 1959).
5. Master Eckhart, *Das Buch Der Göttlichen Tröstung* (Frankfurt: Insel Verlag, 1987).
6. Jacques Lusseyran, *And There Was Light* (Boston: Little, Brown, 1963).
7. Kireet Joshi, *Sri Aurobindo and the Mother: Glimpses of Their Experiments, Experiences, and Realizations.* (New Delhi: Mother's Institute of Research in Association with Motilal Banarsidass, Delhi, 1989).
8. Eike Braunroth, *Heute Schon Eine Schnecke Geküsst? Grundlagenwerk Der Kooperation Mit Der Natur* (Frankeneck: Wega, 2002).
9. Alice Miller, *For Your Own Good: Hidden Cruelty in Child-rearing and the Roots of Violence* (New York: Farrar, Straus, Giroux, 1983).
10. Wilhelm Reich, *The Mass Psychology of Fascism* (New York: Farrar, Straus & Giroux, 1970).

11. Dietrich Bonhoeffer, *Ethics*. (New York: Macmillan, 1955).

Chapter 6: What Will Happen After the Collapse of the Globalized Systems?

1. Dorothy Maclean, *To Hear the Angels Sing: An Odyssey of Co-creation with the Devic Kingdom* (Hudson, NY: Lindisfarne, 1994).

Chapter 7: The Inner Operator

1. Satprem and F. De Towarnicki, *My Burning Heart* (New York, NY: Institute for Evolutionary Research, 1989).
2. Lao Tzu, *Tao Te Ching* (Milano: Mondadori, 2001).
3. Karl O. Schmidt, *So Heilt Der Geist! Wesen U. Dynamik D. Geistigen Heilens* (München: Drei-Eichen-Verlag, 1984).
4. Makarand R. Paranjape, ed., *The Penguin Sri Aurobindo Reader* (New Delhi: Penguin, 1999).
5. Mark 13:11, *Holy Bible* (New American Standard Bible).

Chapter 8: The Sacred Matrix

1. Martin Maria Schönberger, *The I Ching and the Genetic Code: The Hidden Key to Life* (New York: ASI, 1979).

Chapter 9: The Power of Christ

1. Karl Marx, *Critique of Hegel's Philosophy of Right*, trans. Annette Jolin and Joseph O'Malley, ed. Joseph O'Malley (Cambridge, England: Cambridge University Press, 1970).
2. Pierre Teilhard De Chardin, *The Phenomenon of Man* (New York: Harper Torchbooks, 1959).
3. Ernst Bloch, *The Principle of Hope*. (Cambridge, MA: The MIT Press, 1986).
4. *Ibid.*
5. C.J. Rowe, *Plato: Symposium* (Warminster: Aris & Phillips, 1998).
6. John 4:8, *Holy Bible* (New American Standard Bible).

Chapter 10: Ananda

1. Sepp Holzer and Konrad Liebchen. *Sepp Holzer: The Rebel Farmer.* (Graz: Stocker, 2004).

Chapter 11: The Holy Land

1. Ryan Stone, "The Art of Amarna: Akhenaten and His Life under the Sun." *Ancient Origins* (January 20, 2015), last accessed July 19, 2015, http://www.ancient-origins.net/ancient-places-africa/art-amarna-akhenaten-and-his-life-under-sun-002587.
2. Dieter Duhm, *The Sacred Matrix: From the Matrix of Violence to the Matrix of Life; the Foundation for a New Civilization* (Wiesenburg: Verlag Meiga, 2008).
3. Theodor Herzl, *If You Will It, It Is No Fairytale* (Jerusalem: Wzo, 1954).

Chapter 12: Water, Food, and Energy are Freely Available to Humankind

1. John D. Liu, "Learning to Communicate the Lessons of the Loess Plateau" (Environmental Education Media Project, 2007), *academia.edu*, last accessed July 19, 2015, https://www.academia.edu/12899656/Learning_to_Communicate_the_Lessons_of_the_Loess_Plateau.
2. CNN, "Water Gandhi," *YouTube* (March 20, 2013), last accessed July 19, 2015, https://www.youtube.com/watch?v=wgUBy-XmKJc.

Chapter 13: The Reality of the Utopian Goal

1. Ernst Bloch, *The Principle of Hope* (Cambridge, MA: The MIT Press, 1986).
2. *Ibid*.
3. Luke 17:21, *Holy Bible* (New American Standard Bible).
4. Sabine Lichtenfels, *Oracle Trance,* (Tamera, Portugal, September 2011).
5. Jacques Lusseyran, *And There Was Light* (Boston: Little, Brown, 1963).

Chapter 14: Powers of Manifestation

1. Eugen Herrigel, *Zen in the Art of Archery*, trans. R.F.C. Hull (New York: Vintage, 1999).
2. Dhyani Ywahoo, *Am Feuer Der Weisheit: Lehren Der Cherokee-Indianer* (Zürich: Theseus, 1988).
3. Martin Winiecki, "The Miracle of Mulatos: A Centre for Planetary Future in the Colombian Jungle," trans. Marina Köhler, *The Peace*

Village San Jose Must Live!, 2011, http://www.sos-sanjose.org/uploads/media/Mulatos_e.pdf.
4. Herrigel, *Zen in the Art of Archery.*
5. Lao Tsu and Bart Marshall, *Tao Te Ching: A New English Version* (Bart Marshall, 2006), last accessed July 26 2015, http://www.scribd.com/doc/7544192/Tao-Te-Ching-Bart-Marshall#scribd.
6. Meister Eckhart and Maurice O'C. Walshe, *The Complete Mystical Works of Meister Eckhart* (New York: Crossroad Publishing Company, 2010).
7. Satprem and F. De Towarnicki, *My Burning Heart* (New York, NY: Institute for Evolutionary Research, 1989).
8. Lao Tsu and Bart Marshall, *Tao Te Ching: A New English Version.*
9. Peace Pilgrim, *Steps toward Inner Peace: Harmonious Principles for Human Living* (Santa Fe, NM: Ocean Tree Books, 1992).

Chapter 15: The Earth Needs New Information

1. David Bohm, *Wholeness and the Implicate Order* (London, Boston: Routledge & Kegan Paul, 1980).
2. Dieter Duhm, "Global Campus," *Setting Foundations for a New Civilization: Perspectives for the Global Revolution. A Collection of Study Materials from the Terra Nova School,* ed. Martin Winiecki (Belzig: Verlag Meiga, 2013), 37.

Chapter 16: Healing in the Spirit of Oneness

1. Albert Einstein, "Letter of 1950," as quoted in *The New York Times* (March 29, 1972) and *The New York Post* (November 28, 1972), according to www.wikiquote.org, last accessed July 26, 2015. NOTE: Wikiquotes states that the original letter is "a different and presumably more accurate version."
2. Jurgen Dahl, *Der unbegreifliche Garten und seine Verwustung: Uber Okologie und uber Okologie hinaus* (Stuttgart: Klett-Cotta, 1984).
3. Johann Wolfgang von Goethe, "Introduction," *Theory of Colors,* trans. Charles L. Eastlake (New York: Dover Publications, 2006).
4. Henri J. M. Nouwen, *The Return of the Prodigal Son: A Story of Homecoming* (New York: Image Books, 1994).
5. K. O. Schmidt, *Sei Geheilt!: Die Heilwunder Jesu - Auch Heute Möglich!* (Pforzheim: Frick, 1975).

Chapter 17: It is Life Itself that Heals

1. Jacques Lusseyran, *And There Was Light* (Boston: Little, Brown, 1963).
2. Arcady Petrov, *Save Yourself. Part I of Trilogy Creation of the Universe* (Hamburg: Jelezky, 2011).
3. Sepp Holzer and Bernd Mueller, "Water Is Life - The Water Retention Landscape of Tamera," *YouTube*, (September 14, 2011), last accessed July 26, 2015, https://www.youtube.com/watch?v=4hF2QL0D5ww.

Chapter 18: Healing by Activating the Original Matrix

1. Lichtenfels, Sabine. *Traumsteine Reise in Das Zeitalter Der Sinnlichen Erfüllung*. (Kreuzlingen: Hugendubel, 2000).
2. Joseph Von Eichendorff, *Werke in sechs Bänden - Band 1* (Frankfurt: Deutscher Klassiker Verlag, 1987).
3. Ruth Pfau, *Verrückter Kann Man Gar Nicht Leben: Ärztin, Nonne, Powerfrau* (Freiburg: Verlag Herder GmbH, 2013).
4. Jacques Lusseyran, *And There Was Light* (Boston: Little, Brown, 1963).

Chapter 19: The Healing of Love

1. Elisabeth Kübler-Ross, *Über Den Tod Und Das Leben Danach* (Güllesheim: Silberschnur Verlag, 2010).
2. Clarissa Pinkola Estes, *Women Who Run with the Wolves: Myths and Stories of the Wild Woman Archetype* (New York: Ballantine Books, 1992).
3. Lao Tzu, *Tao Te Ching* (Milano: Mondadori, 2001).
4. John 1:14, *Holy Bible* (New American Standard Bible).
5. Genesis 4:1, *Holy Bible* (New American Standard Bible).
6. Sabine Lichtenfels, *Weiche Macht: Perspektiven Eines Neuen Frauenbewusstseins Und Einer Neuen Liebe Zu Den Männern* (Belzig: Berghoff and Friends, 1996).
7. Pierre Teilhard De Chardin and Othon Marbach, *Der Mensch Im Kosmos* (München: C. H. Beck Verlag, 1959).

Chapter 20: Liberating Sexuality

1. Arthur Schopenhauer and E. F. J. Payne, *The World as Will and Representation* (New York: Dover Publications, 1966).

2. Pierre Teilhard De Chardin, *Das Herz Der Materie* (Olten: Walter Verlag, 1990).
3. Douglas Carlton Abrams, *The Lost Diary of Don Juan: An Account of the True Arts of Passion and the Perilous Adventure of Love* (New York: Atria Books, 2007).
4. Wilhelm Reich, *Volume 1 of The Discovery of the Orgone: The Function of the Orgasm: Sex-Economic Problems of Biological Energy* (New York: Farrar, Straus and Giroux, 1973).
5. Wilhelm Reich, *The Cancer Biopathy* (New York: Farrar, Straus and Giroux, 1973).
6. Sabine Lichtenfels, *Traumsteine. Reise in Das Zeitalter Der Sinnlichen Erfüllung* (Kreuzlingen: Hugendubel, 2000).
7. Sabine Kleinhammes, *Rettet Den Sex: Ein Manifest Von Frauen Für Einen Neuen Sexuellen Humanismus* (Radolfzell: Verlag Meiga, 1988).

Chapter 21: Objective Ethics

1. Jacques Lusseyran, *Against the Pollution of the I: Selected Writings of Jacques Lusseyran* (New York: Parabola Books, 1999).
2. Pierre Teilhard De Chardin, *The Phenomenon of Man* (New York: Harper Torchbooks, 1959).
3. Sabine Lichtenfels, *Sources of Love and Peace* (Belzig: Verlag Meiga, 2004).
4. Matthew 7:1, *Holy Bible* (New American Standard Bible).
5. Sabine Lichtenfels, *Grace: Pilgrimage for a Future without War* (Wiesenburg: Verlag Meiga, 2007).

Chapter 22: What is Peace?

1. Sabine Lichtenfels, *Sources of Love and Peace.* (Belzig: Verlag Meiga, 2004).
2. Peace Pilgrim, *Steps toward Inner Peace: Harmonious Principles for Human Living* (Santa Fe, NM: Ocean Tree Books, 1992).
3. *Ibid.*

Chapter 24: Creating Functioning Communities

1. Richard Wilhelm and Cary F. Baynes, *The I Ching; Or, Book of Changes* (Princeton, NJ: Princeton University Press, 1967).
2. John Briggs and F. David Peat, *Turbulent Mirror: An Illustrated Guide to Chaos Theory and the Science of Wholeness* (New York: Perennial Library / Harper & Row, 1990).

3. Eike Braunroth, *Heute Schon Eine Schnecke Geküsst? Kooperation Mit Der Natur* (Frankeneck: Wega, 2002).
4. Hermann Löns, *Kraut Und Lot: Ein Buch Für Jäger U. Heger* (Radebeul: Neumann, 1955).
5. Sabine Lichtenfels, *Traumsteine. Reise in Das Zeitalter Der Sinnlichen Erfüllung* (Kreuzlingen: Hugendubel, 2000).
6. Sabine Lichtenfels, Sabine, *Temple of Love a Journey into the Age of Sensual Fulfillment* (Belzig: Verlag Meiga, 2011).
7 Sabine Lichtenfels, *Traumsteine. Reise in Das Zeitalter Der Sinnlichen Erfüllung* (Kreuzlingen: Hugendubel, 2000).
8. Wolf-Dieter Storl, *Streifzüge Am Rande Midgards* (Burgrain: Koha-Verlag GmbH, 2006).

Chapter 25: The Sacred Alliance of Life

1. Isaiah 11:6-9, *Holy Bible* (New American Standard Bible).
2. Wilhelm Reich, *The Murder of Christ: The Emotional Plague of Mankind* (New York: Farrar, Straus and Giroux, 1953).
3. Jim Nollman, *The Man Who Talks to Whales: the Art of Interspecies Communication* (Boulder, CO: Sentient Publications, 2002).
4. Eike Braunroth, *Heute Schon Eine Schnecke Geküsst? Kooperation Mit Der Natur* (Frankeneck: Wega, 2002).

Chapter 28: The Secret of Water

1. Olof Alexandersson, *Living Water: Viktor Schauberger and the Secrets of Natural Energy* (Wellow: Gateway, 1979).
2. Viktor Schauberger and Jörg Schauberger, *Das Wesen Des Wassers* (Baden: AT-Verl., 2006).
3. Theodor Schwenk and Wolfram Schwenk, *Water: The Element of Life: Essays* (Hudson, NY: Anthroposophic, 1989).
4. Masaru Emoto, *The Secret Life of Water* (New York: Atria, 2005).
5. Sepp Holzer and Bernd Mueller, "Water Is Life - The Water Retention Landscape of Tamera," *YouTube* (September 14, 2011), last accessed August 15, 2015, https://www.youtube.com/watch?v=4hF2QL0D5ww.

Chapter 29: Religion – The Existence of the Divine World

1. Olof Alexandersson, *Living Water: Viktor Schauberger and the Secrets of Natural Energy* (Wellow: Gateway, 1979).

2. Francisco Cândido Xavier and André Luiz. *Nosso Lar* (Rio De Janeiro, Brazil: Federação Espírita Brasileira, 2005).
3. Útmutató a Léleknek,. "Do You Believe in Mother?" *Cranach: The Blog of Veith* (February 9, 2015), last accessed August 15, 2015, http://www.patheos.com/blogs/geneveith/2015/02/do-you-believe-in-mother/.
4. Prentice Mulford, *Unfug Des Lebens Und Des Sterbens* (Frankfurt Am Main: Fischer Taschenbuch Verlag GmbH, 1977).
5. Meister Eckhart, *The Complete Mystical Works of Meister Eckhart,* trans. Maurice O'C. Walshe (New York: Crossroad Publishing Company, 2010).
6. K. O. Schmidt, *So Heilt Der Geist!: Wesen Und Dynamik Des Geistigen Heilens* (Engelberg: Drei-Eichen-Verlag, 1978).

Chapter 30: Political Theory

1. Victor Hugo, *History of a Crime (Deposition of a Witness),* trans. Huntington Smith (New York: T.Y. Crowell, 1888).

Chapter 31: The Tamera Project

1. Dieter Duhm, et al., *Setting Foundations for a New Civilization: Perspectives for the Global Revolution. A Collection of Study Materials from the Terra Nova School* (Belzig: Verlag Meiga, 2013).
2. Leila Dregger, *Tamera: A Model for the Future* (Belzig: Verlag Meiga, 2010).

Glossary

1. C.J. Rowe, *Plato: Symposium* (Warminster: Aris & Phillips, 1998).
2. Ervin Laszlo, *The Akashic Experience: Science and the Cosmic Memory Field* (Rochester, VT: Inner Traditions, 2009).
3. Carlos Castaneda, *The Power of Silence: Further Lessons of Don Juan* (New York: Simon and Schuster, 1987).
4. Wilhelm Reich, *Character Analysis* (New York: Farrar, Straus and Giroux, 1980).
5. Wilhelm Reich, *The Murder of Christ: The Emotional Plague of Mankind* (New York: Farrar, Straus and Giroux, 1953).
6. Ernst Bloch, *Zur Ontologie Des Noch-Nicht-Seins. Ein Vortrag Und Zwei Abhandlungen* (Frankfurt/a.M.: Suhrkamp Verlag, 1961).
7. Dorothy Maclean, *To Hear the Angels Sing: An Odyssey of Co-creation with the Devic Kingdom* (Hudson, NY: Lindisfarne, 1994).

8. Aristotle, *On the Soul. Parva Naturalia. On Breath,* trans. W. S. Hett (London: W. Heinemann, 1957).
9. Werner Heisenberg, *Physics and Philosophy: The Revolution in Modern Science* (New York: Harper & Brothers, 1958).
10. Michael Talbot, *The Holographic Universe* (New York: Harper Perennial, 1992).
11. David Bohm, *Wholeness and the Implicate Order* (London, Boston: Routledge & Kegan Paul, 1980).
12. Rupert Sheldrake, *Morphic Resonance: The Nature of Formative Causation* (Rochester, VT: Park Street Press, 2009).
13. Pierre Teilhard De Chardin, *The Phenomenon of Man* (New York: Harper Torchbooks, 1959).
14. Wilhelm Reich, *The Discovery of the Orgone: The Function of the Orgasm* (New York: Noonday, 1961).
15. Dieter Duhm, The Sacred Matrix: From the Matrix of Violence to the Matrix of Life; the Foundation for a New Civilization (Wiesenburg: Verlag Meiga, 2008).
16. Sri Aurobindo, *The Supramental Manifestation upon Earth* (Pondicherry: Sri Aurobindo Ashram, 1952).
17. Śankara and Ānanda Girī, *The Chāndogya Upanishad* (Osnabrück: Biblio Verlag, 1980).
18. Bernd Walter Mueller, "The Secret of Water as a Basis for the New Earth," *Tamera.org* (May 2011) last accessed August 15, 2015, http://www.tamera.org/fileadmin/PDF/WasserSymposium_en.pdf.
19. Aristotle, *Politik,* trans. Eckart Schütrumpf (Berlin: Akademie-Verlag, 1991).